CRazy at the Cabin

A Cozy Collection of Crazy-Pieced Quilts

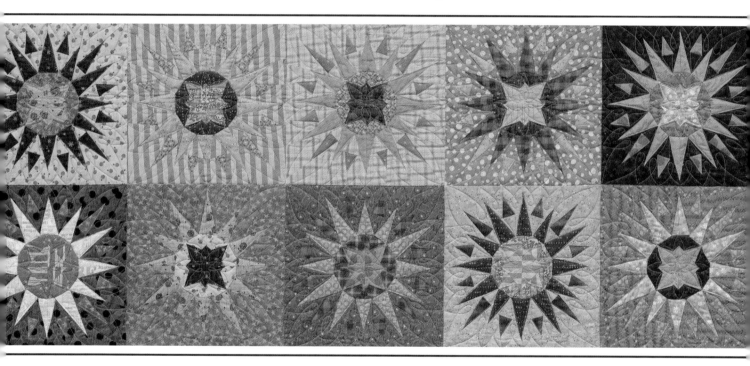

Janet Rae Nesbitt

Martingale
Create with Confidence

Crazy at the Cabin: A Cozy Collection of Crazy-Pieced Quilts
© 2016 by Janet Rae Nesbitt

Martingale®
19021 120th Ave. NE, Ste. 102
Bothell, WA 98011-9511 USA
ShopMartingale.com

Printed in China
21 20 19 18 17 16   8 7 6 5 4 3 2 1

Library of Congress Cataloging-in-Publication Data
is available upon request.

ISBN: 978-1-60468-783-5

MISSION STATEMENT

We empower makers who use fabric and yarn
to make life more enjoyable.

CREDITS

PUBLISHER AND
CHIEF VISIONARY OFFICER
Jennifer Erbe Keltner

CONTENT DIRECTOR
Karen Costello Soltys

DESIGN MANAGER
Adrienne Smitke

MANAGING EDITOR
Tina Cook

PRODUCTION MANAGER
Regina Girard

ACQUISITIONS EDITOR
Karen M. Burns

COVER AND
INTERIOR DESIGNER
Connor Chin

TECHNICAL EDITOR
Nancy Mahoney

PHOTOGRAPHER
Brent Kane

COPY EDITOR
Sheila Chapman Ryan

ILLUSTRATOR
Christine Erikson

SEPTEMBER 2016

CONTENTS

INTRODUCTION 4
GENERAL CRAZINESS 5

 Wish upon a (Crazy) Star 12

 Crazy Sand Dollars 20

 Crazy Summer Blooms 24

 Crazy Hot 28

 What a Hoot! 33

 Crazy Regatta 50

 Welcome to the Lake 61

 Crazy Moose Messages 71

 Folk-Art Fireworks 80

 Cabins in the Pines 88

ABOUT THE AUTHOR 96

INTRODUCTION

I'm a rule follower. I've always been one, so it comes as no surprise that I have a list of "rules" for life at the lake cabin. Rules like *Have fun in the sun*. That's easy—I can check that off my list! *Go jump in the lake* and *Go boating:* check and check! And there's *Take a walk on the beach*, *Collect interesting shells and rocks*, and *Enjoy the wildlife*, check, check, and check! *Watch the sunset*, *Stay up late*, *Watch the fireworks*, and *Wish upon a star*. Check, check, and double check!

If I can manage to check all these off my list, then it's an automatic check for the all-important *Make memories* rule. Yup, I'm a rule follower, but weekend rules at the lake cabin are some of the easiest rules to adhere to. So go ahead—be a little crazy. Break a rule or two, but here's one you're not going to want to skip: *Enjoy!*

GENERAL CRAZINESS

I call my quilts and techniques "Crazies" because they're a little wonky, a little mixed up, but a whole lot of fun. Over the years, I've designed too many Crazy-pieced quilts to count. You may already be a longtime fan, or this may be your first attempt at my technique, so here's where you'll find the basic how-to information on the process of stacking, cutting, and shuffling the fabric pieces to make similar but no-two-the-same blocks for your quilt projects. First we'll take a look at how to do this type of Crazy piecing, and then I'll show you how I like to add appliqué elements to my quilts using wool.

This section explains the method to my madness, especially for anyone who may be making one of my Crazies for the very first time. The first thing you need to know is that one piece of fabric will make one block. If you need nine blocks, start with nine fabrics. It couldn't be easier. It's a breeze to make any of these quilts larger or smaller; all you have to do is change the number of fabrics you start with so you can make more or fewer blocks accordingly.

We'll go over how to stack the fabrics first, then I'll show you an example of how to make a Crazy block, from trading or shuffling the fabrics to sewing the blocks. Let's get started!

ABOUT STACKING

The way I create the Crazy effect is to stack all my fabrics together, cut the pieces all at once, and then either trade or shuffle the pieces to mix things up. When it comes to stacking the fabrics, put them all right sides up. *Right sides up!* I can never say that enough when I'm teaching any Crazy class. That's the most important thing to remember. But here are some additional pointers for stacking your fabrics, depending on the final look you're going for.

Stacking for scrappy blocks. Stacking is fairly easy when the quilt is going to be totally scrappy, with different fabric in each position in the block, and you're stacking in two (or more) color piles, i.e. lights and darks. When stacking for these types of quilt patterns, just make sure that **ALL** of the lights contrast with **ALL** of the darks. I audition my darkest light against each of the darks and my lightest dark against each light. Then make sure the fabrics in each stack have contrast from each other by color, print design, print size, and/or type as you stack.

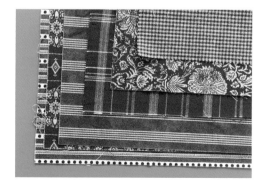
Take a photo of the order of fabrics for reference.

Stacking fabrics for planned blocks. Stacking can be more challenging when the blocks aren't totally scrappy and have a set number of fabrics per block, such as two, three, four, or even more fabrics per block, such as in the Owl block below.

Stacking for a planned color scheme. It's easier if you have a color scheme; you can follow it for stacking purposes. For example: red, white, blue; red, white, blue; until all the fabrics are stacked. Stacking can get trickier if you don't have a color scheme and want to use a wide variety of medium or dark fabrics, so let's look at an example.

The owl (quilt is on page 34) uses three medium to dark fabrics per block

LET'S TRY A STACKING EXAMPLE

Begin by counting the number of elements in the block to determine how many fabrics will be together as you stack. "What a Hoot" on page 33 and shown above has fabric #1 for the owl, fabric #2 for the owl's stomach, and fabric #3 for the background; so every three fabrics will be together in a block. The

5

sailboat from "Crazy Regatta" on page 50 has fabric #1 for the sail, fabric #2 for the mast and boat stripe, fabric #3 for the boat and flag, and fabric #4 for the background; so you need to look at every four fabrics for those blocks. The following example is for making blocks with three elements.

1. Select three fabrics that you want to use together in a block and stack #1 on the bottom, #2 in the middle, and #3 on top. Each fabric must contrast with both of the other fabrics as these will appear in the same block.

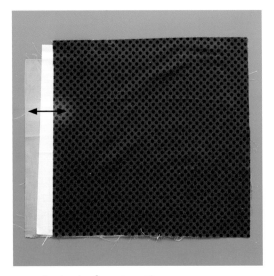

A stack of contrasting squares.

2. Add a fourth fabric that looks good with the group, but most importantly that contrasts with fabrics #2 and #3 because the top three fabrics will appear together in a block.

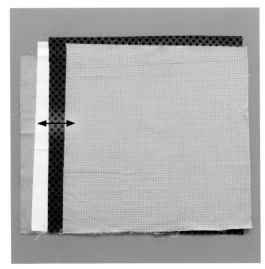

Add a fourth fabric to the stack.

3. Add a fifth fabric to the top of the stack that looks good with the group and contrasts with fabrics #3 and #4. (By now you see that the new fabric will always be used with the two fabrics right below it.)

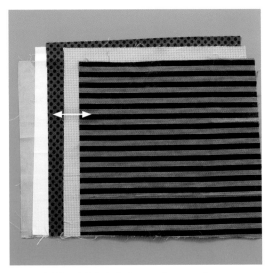

Add a fifth fabric to the stack.

4. Keep going until all fabrics are stacked. If you're left with one or two fabrics that don't contrast, you still have time to fit them into your stack before you cut. Check the fabrics on the top of the stack to be sure they contrast with the fabrics on the bottom of the stack, because once you shuffle them, the top fabric will be paired with fabrics #1 and #2 from the bottom of the stack and the top two fabrics will be paired with fabric #1. In the example below, the light print on top has to contrast not only with the navy stripe and orange check but also with the green and white fabrics on the bottom of the stack.

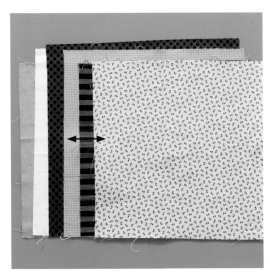

The top fabric on the stack.

For blocks that have four or more elements, stack in the same way, but make sure the first four fabrics have contrast, then 2–5 have contrast, and so on.

BASIC STEPS FOR MAKING A CRAZY BLOCK

1. Stack **all** the fabric right side up for cutting. I can cut as many as 12 to 15 stacked fabrics at one time using a 60 mm rotary cutter. (That's the jumbo size, if you're wondering.) Starting with a new blade makes cutting stacked fabrics even easier. As you stack, try to align two adjacent sides of the fabrics. I align the selvage and the left side of each fabric.

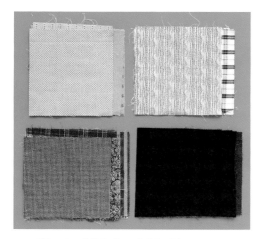

Stack all fabrics right side up.

2. Using a pencil and a ruler, trace the pattern in the book onto the uncoated side of a piece of freezer paper, making sure to label each piece as indicated. Press the freezer-paper pattern onto the top fabric on the stacked fabrics with an iron.

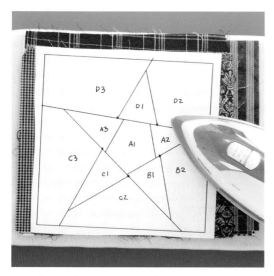

Trace the pattern and press it on top of each fabric stack.

TRADE VS. SHUFFLE

Some blocks require you to trade a whole stack of pieces for another; for other blocks, you'll shuffle individual pieces. Occasionally, you'll do both! The directions will tell you when to trade and when to shuffle. Here's a quick explanation of what to do when you see each phrase.

*When you **trade** pieces, you'll move the whole stack of a specified pattern piece from one stack to another so that each element is a different color group. For example, you'll put the red A1 pieces in the blue stack and the blue A1 pieces in the red stack.*

*When you **shuffle** the pattern pieces, you'll rearrange the individual pieces within each stack. For example, for the A1 pieces, you'll move the top fabric to the bottom of the stack. For A2, you might move two pieces from the top to the bottom of the stack.*

3. Cutting through the freezer paper and the entire stack of fabric, cut on the outer line all around the pattern to remove the excess fabric around the outer edges.

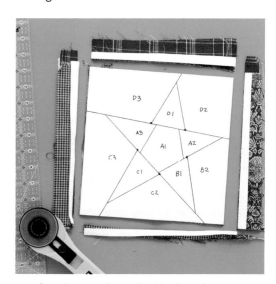

Cut the stack on the block outline.

4. After following the specifics for each block, such as cutting the top half of the block from the bottom half of the block, cut the pattern into sections. The cutting order is determined by saying the alphabet backward and counting backward to determine which section or piece to cut next. For example, if the block is constructed of sections A–F, you'll cut section F from the stack first, then you'll cut section E, followed by section D, and so on.

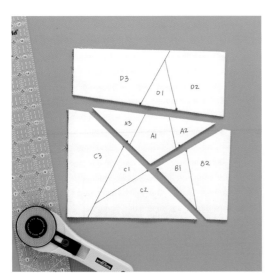

Cut the stack into the lettered sections.

5. Next you'll cut each section into individual pieces by counting backward. If there are three pieces in each section, start by cutting piece 3 from the section first. As you cut out each piece, stack the pieces on the master pattern to keep the pieces organized and oriented correctly.

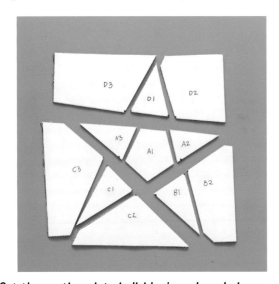

Cut the sections into individual numbered pieces.

6. Once all the pieces are cut apart on the pattern lines and stacked on the master, it's time to shuffle! Remove the freezer paper from the pieces. Then following the instructions for the block you're making, shuffle the fabrics. To make the Wish upon a (Crazy) Star block (page 12), for example, you'd trade an entire stack of pieces from one stack to another so that each element (star points, star center, background) is a different color group.

Trade the fabrics.

SECURE THE PIECES

Once the pieces have been traded or shuffled, pin each stack in place onto a piece of cardboard to secure them until you have a chance to sew all the blocks. That way if the stack is bumped or a breeze blows in the window your pieces won't be scattered.

7. Join the pieces in each alphabetical section in numerical order using a ¼" seam allowance. Start by sewing piece 1 to piece 2. Then add piece 3 to piece 1/2, and so on. Because the pattern is cut apart on the lines **without** adding seam allowances, the pieces won't fit back together perfectly. That's what makes them Crazies! There are dots on the master pattern to indicate which end of the pieces to align. Before sewing two pieces together, look at the pattern to see where the dot is and align the pieces at the end with the dot. Referring to "The Goldilocks Rule" on page 10, sew the pieces together using a ¼" seam allowance. Don't worry if the pieces don't line up at the other end of the seam after stitching. If there are no dots, just center one piece on top of the other piece and stitch.

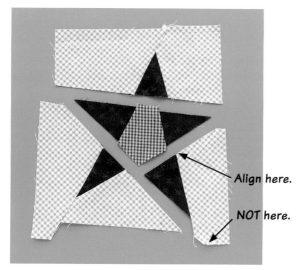

Join the pieces in each alphabetical section, sewing them in numerical order (1 to 2, 1/2 to 3, and so on).

STRAIGHTENING THE EDGES

When straightening the edges, it's important that the portion you trim off is parallel to your ruler so you don't change the angles of the pattern. If there's a funny angle sticking out, go back to your master pattern and check to see if you twisted a piece before you stitched. Don't just trim it off!

8. After each section is pieced, join the sections in alphabetical order: sew section A to section B, then add section C to A/B, and so on. *Before stitching two sections together, you'll need to*

*straighten the edges, trimming off the **least** amount possible.* Generally, the portion that you trim off will be parallel to your ruler. This is a very important step and ensures that the blocks will be flat. For instance, before stitching section A to section B, lay your ruler along the inside edge of section A and trim so that each section has a straight edge for sewing. Repeat for section B. Straighten only the edges you'll sew together.

Trim only the edges to be joined.

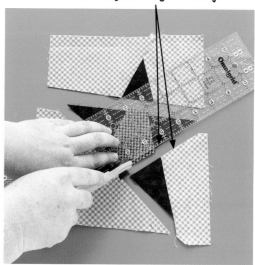

Trim the uneven edge before joining sections.
*Do **not** trim all edges!*

Join the trimmed sections.

9. Trim and join the next section in alphabetical order. For instance, to join section C to section A/B, trim the edges in the same manner as step 8, and then place the sections right sides together. Center the pieces and match the seam intersections as best you can (see "Matching

Diagonal Seams" below); sew the seam. Continue trimming and joining the remaining sections.

Join the next section in alphabetical order.

The specifics for each block—where to match and what to line up—are found in each pattern. Please read the directions prior to starting. I encourage you to make practice blocks using scrap fabric before you cut into your "good stuff" so that you can see how the block is stitched together. Simply count the elements in each block to arrive at the minimum number of fabrics needed to do a test. For the star you need one fabric for the star points and center and a second for the background, so the minimum number of Star blocks you can make with this method is two.

MATCHING DIAGONAL SEAMS—

It can be difficult to match diagonal seams, in comparison to those that naturally butt together, and usually the seams we're trying to match are those pesky diagonal ones! To match diagonal seams, I place the two sections right sides together where I think the seams will match. Then before stitching, I fold back the seam allowance on the top piece a scant 1/4" and peek to see how I did. If the seams match, I pin and sew the seam. If not, I slide the top piece in the direction it needs to go until the seams match. Then I pin and stitch. Good enough for Crazies!

THE GOLDILOCKS RULE

When you align two pieces where you see dots on the pattern, you'll need to have a "dog-ear" sticking up. It can be difficult to decide how large the dog-ear should be. The stitches should go exactly through the point where the two fabrics intersect. The photos show you my Goldilocks rule: instead of being too big or too small, you want the dog-ear to be just right! If the dog-ear is too large or too small, the triangles won't align correctly. The dog-ear below is too large. See how the stitching is just on the striped fabric at the pointed end? The dog-ear to the right is just right since the stitching goes right through the point where the two fabrics meet. Follow this rule wherever there's a dot on the pattern!

The top triangle is too far up, making the dog-ear too large.

The 1/4" seam should go exactly where the fabrics intersect.

When the triangles are aligned correctly, the dog-ear is just right.

FUSIBLE WOOL APPLIQUÉ

Some of the projects in this book feature wool appliqué, which is fun and easy to do. You don't need to turn under the edges as you go because wool won't fray like cotton. The pattern pieces are all facing as in the finished quilts. If you want to fuse the pieces, you'll need to reverse the patterns first. Or follow my process to make fused appliqués without tracing the patterns backward.

1. Press lightweight, paper-backed fusible web onto the wrong side of a piece of wool, following the manufacturer's directions.

2. Carefully remove the paper backing from the piece of wool, trying to keep the paper intact without tearing. You'll be tracing the appliqué shape onto the glue side of the paper. As you separate the paper from the wool, pretend you're opening a book; on one side is the wool with the glue side up and on the other side is the paper backing with the tracing side facing up.

3. Using a permanent black marker, trace the motifs onto the paper backing. Place the paper backing back on the wool with the marked side of the backing and the glue on the wool together. Press the paper backing in place with an iron; this will "transfer" the traced shape onto the glue side of the wool.

4. After the wool has cooled, remove the paper backing again and cut out the shapes. Be sure to leave a very scant ¼" of fabric on any edge that needs to tuck underneath another shape. For example, in "Crazy Moose Messages" (page 71), the jack-o-lantern and face go under the jack-o-lantern inside so you need a scant ¼" at the top of the jack-o-lantern to tuck under the inside piece.

5. Once all the motifs have been cut out, place an appliqué pressing sheet on top of the full-sized pattern. Using the pattern for a placement guide, lay the appliqué pieces in place on top of the pressing sheet, tucking the leaves under the stems and the stems under the flowers, etc. Using a wool setting on your iron, fuse the pieces together **only** where they overlap. Allow to cool.

6. After the design has cooled, carefully remove it from the pressing sheet. Place the entire design on the right side of the background, with the glue side down. Fuse the entire design in place.

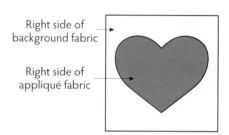

7. Whipstitch all of the appliqué pieces in place using wool thread or a thread of your choosing to match each piece. Once the design has been stitched, press the block from the wrong side. Trim the block to the desired size, if required.

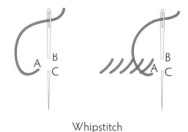

Whipstitch

Wish upon a (Crazy) Star

It's always such a thrill to see a shooting star. At the lake, away from the city lights, chances are high that we may just get to take Jiminy Cricket's advice and wish upon a star! Here's hoping that you'll get to see a shooting star—and may all your dreams come true.

MATERIALS

Yardage is based on 42"-wide fabric. Fat quarters measure 18" x 21".

2⅞ yards of taupe linen for Hourglass blocks, inner border, and outer border

6 fat quarters *each* of assorted medium-red and dark-red prints for Star blocks, Hourglass blocks, and checkerboard border (12 total)

⅞ yard of cream-and-tan check linen for Hourglass blocks and checkerboard border

6 fat quarters of assorted cream prints for Star blocks

5 fat quarters of assorted tan prints for Star blocks

1 fat quarter of tan stripe for Star block and Hourglass blocks

¾ yard of red stripe for binding

4 yards of fabric for backing

68" x 80" piece of batting

Freezer paper

CUTTING

From *each* of the medium-red and dark-red prints, cut:

1 square, 11" x 11" (12 total)

From the remaining medium-red and dark-red prints, cut a *total* of:

16 squares, 7¼" x 7¼"; cut each square into quarters diagonally to yield 64 triangles (2 will be extra)

11 rectangles, 2½" x 14"

2 squares, 2½" x 2½"

From *each* of the cream and tan prints, cut:

1 square, 11" x 11" (11 total)

From the tan stripe, cut:

1 square, 11" x 11"

2 squares, 7¼" x 7¼"; cut each square into quarters diagonally to yield 8 triangles

From the cream-and-tan check linen, cut:

2 strips, 7¼" x 42"; crosscut into 10 squares, 7¼" x 7¼". Cut each square into quarters diagonally to yield 40 triangles.

4 strips, 2½" x 42"; crosscut into:

11 rectangles, 2½" x 14"

2 squares, 2½" x 2½"

From the taupe linen, cut:

1 strip, 7¼" x 42"; crosscut into 4 squares, 7¼" x 7¼". Cut each square into quarters diagonally to yield 16 triangles (2 will be extra).

10 strips, 6½" x 42"; cut 3 *of the* strips into 14 squares, 6½" x 6½"

6 strips, 2½" x 42"

From the red stripe, cut:

8 strips, 2½" x 42"

MAKING THE CRAZY STAR BLOCKS

Before you begin, see "General Craziness" on page 5 for detailed instructions.

1. Stack the six cream 11" squares in a pile, right side up. Repeat to make a second pile of six tan and tan-striped squares. Make a third pile of six medium-red squares and a fourth pile of six dark-red squares. All of the fabrics in *each* pile must be right side up. As you stack, align the bottom and left side of *each* square.

Made by Gloria Brodhagen and quilted by Karen Brown.

Finished size: 62½" x 74½" • **Block size: 6" x 6"**

PLAN AHEAD

Typically with Crazy blocks it's difficult to predict which fabrics will end up together in the same block, but with this block it's easier to see! The bottom fabrics of each pile will be together in one of four blocks. Then the next layer of cream, tan, medium red, and dark red (all of the fabrics second from the bottom) will be together in one of four blocks. So look at each layer as you stack them up to make sure you like your combination of fabrics.

2. Trace the Star pattern on pages 18 and 19 seven times (one for each stack of fabric plus three extra to stack on) onto the uncoated side of a piece of freezer paper. Be sure trace all lines and to label each section. Press a freezer-paper pattern onto the top of each stack of squares.

3. Using a rotary cutter and ruler, cut the block from each stack, cutting through the freezer paper and the entire stack of fabric. Note that the sections are labeled alphabetically. Start cutting at the letter closest to the end of the alphabet and work backward until you get to A. (I say the alphabet backward and count backward to determine the cutting order.) Continue cutting until all the individual pieces have been separated. As you cut out each piece, stack each color on its own master so you still have four stacks of fabric, each a different color.

4. Remove the freezer paper from all the pieces. Trade the pieces among the stacks as detailed below until there are four colored stars with a contrasting background in each stack.

- Put all of the dark-red A1 star centers in the cream stack and all of the cream A1 star centers in the dark-red stack. Put the medium-red A1 star centers in the tan stack. Put the tan A1 star centers in the medium-red stack.

- Move the dark-red star points (A2, A3, B1, C1, and D1) to the tan stack. Move the tan star points to the dark-red stack. Put the medium-red star points in the cream stack. Put the cream star points in the medium-red stack.

- All of the background pieces (B2, C2, C3, D2, and D3) stay where they started.

You should now have light stars with red backgrounds and red stars with light backgrounds, and each star should have its companion-colored center (such as cream with tan or medium red with dark red). And, there's no shuffling required.

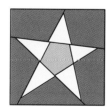

5. To sew the block back together, join the pieces into four sections (A–D) as described below. (See "Matching Diagonal Seams" on page 10). Refer to the pattern to make sure you sew the correct edges together and follow the dots for placement between sections.

- **Section A.** Center A2 on top of A1 and stitch. Center A3 on top of A1/A2 and stitch.

- **Section B.** Stitch B1 to B2, keeping the seam adjacent to section A straight (noted by dot on pattern).

- **Section C.** Stitch C1 to C2, and then add C3, trying to keep the inside seam adjacent to section A straight (noted by dot on pattern). Straighten the C1/C2 edge before adding C3.

- **Section D.** Stitch D1 to D2, and then add D3, trying to keep the inside seam adjacent to section A straight (noted by dot on pattern). Straighten the D1/D2 edge before adding D3.

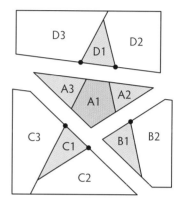

6. Straighten the edges before stitching one section to another section, making sure to only trim the edges you're sewing. Join the sections as follows.

- **Join A and B,** matching the star-point seams.

- **Add C to A/B,** centering the edge of C1 with A1. The seam intersections probably won't match up.

- **Add D to A/B/C,** centering D1 with A1. Again, the seam intersections won't necessarily match.

7. Press and square up the block to measure 6½" x 6½", centering the star.

8. Repeat to make a total of 24 blocks. Only 18 blocks are needed for this project. Save the remaining blocks for another project or use them to piece a cute backing for your quilt.

MAKING THE HOURGLASS BLOCKS

Stitch the 7¼" triangles together as shown on page 16. Press the seam allowances toward the red triangles so the seams will butt into each other. Make 13 red/cream blocks and four red/tan-stripe blocks for the center of the quilt. Make 14 red/cream/taupe blocks for around the edges of the quilt top.

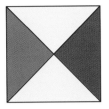

Make 13.

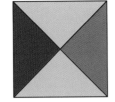

Make 4.

Make 14.

MAKING THE CHECKERBOARD BORDER

1. Sew a red rectangle to the long side of cream-and-tan rectangle to make a strip set as shown. Make 11 strip sets. Crosscut the strip sets into 52 segments, 2½" wide.

2½"

Make 11 strip sets.
Cut 52 segments.

2. Sew 14 segments from step 1 together end to end, beginning with a cream-check square. Sew a cream-check 2½" square to the red end to make a side border. The strip should begin and end with a cream square. Make two side borders.

3. Join 12 segments from step 1 end to end, beginning with a red square. Sew a red 2½" square to the cream end to make the top border. The strip should begin and end with a red square. Repeat to make the bottom border.

ASSEMBLING THE QUILT TOP

1. Lay out the Star blocks, Hourglass blocks, and taupe squares in nine rows of seven blocks each as shown in the quilt assembly diagram on page 17. Sew the blocks together in rows. Press the seam allowances as indicated. Join the rows. Press the seam allowances in one direction.

2. For the inner border, join the taupe 2½"-wide strips end to end. From the pieced strip, cut two 54½"-long strips for the side borders and two 46½"-long strips for the top and bottom borders. Sew the side borders to the quilt top first, and then add the top and bottom borders. Press all seam allowances toward the inner border.

3. Sew the checkerboard borders the sides of the quilt top first, and then add the top and bottom borders. Press all seam allowances toward the inner borders.

4. For the outer border, join the taupe 6½"-wide strips end to end. Cut four 62½"-long strips. Sew the side borders to the quilt top first, and then add the top and bottom borders. Press all seam allowances toward the outer border.

FINISHING THE QUILT

If you need help with any of the following finishing tasks, go to ShopMartingale.com/HowtoQuilt for free, downloadable information. Layer the quilt top with batting and backing; baste. Hand or machine quilt as desired. Use the red-striped 2½"-wide strips to make and attach the binding.

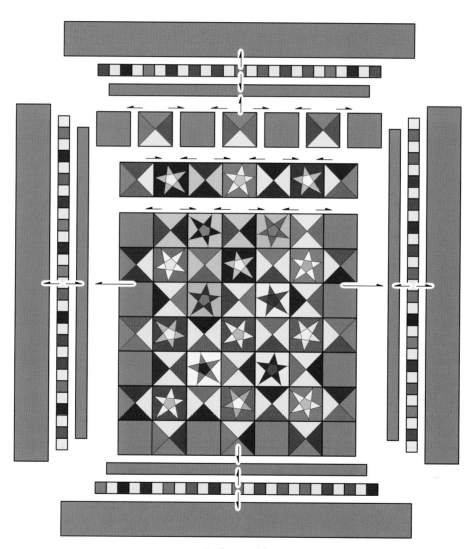

Quilt assembly

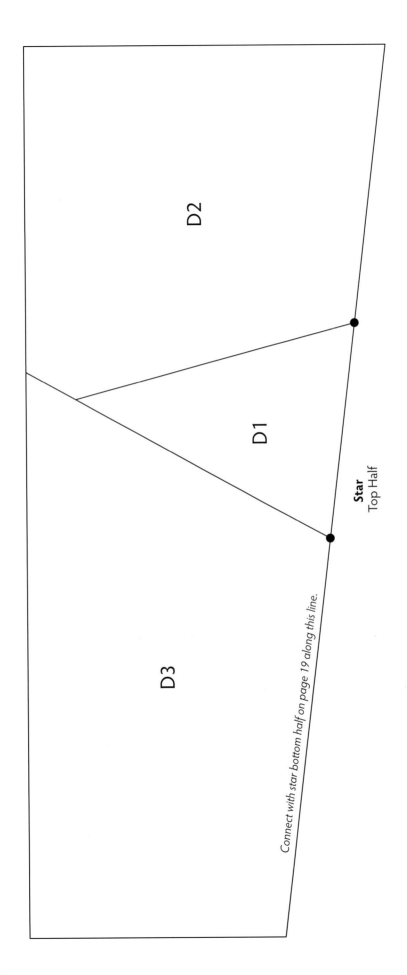

D2

D1

Star
Top Half

D3

Connect with star bottom half on page 19 along this line.

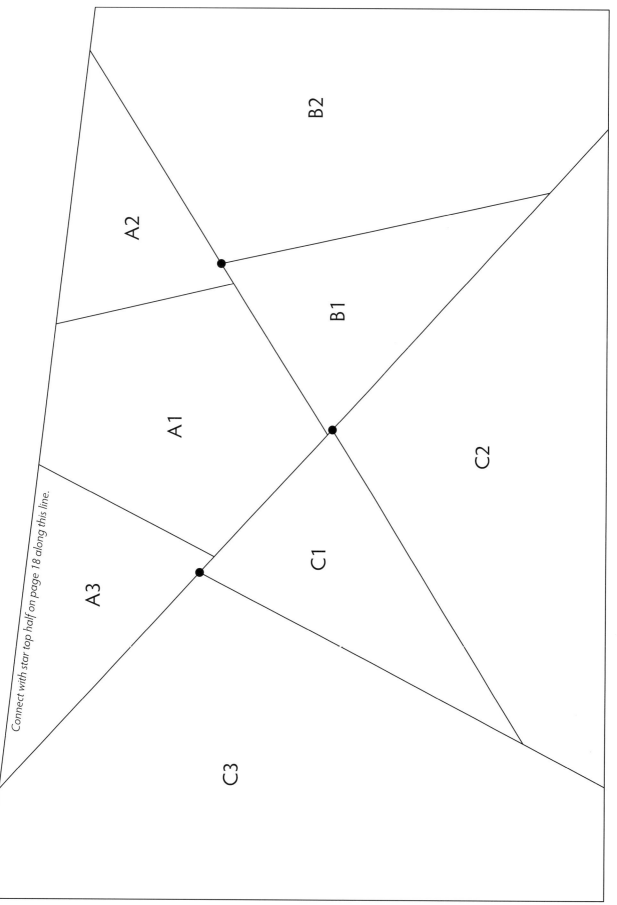

Connect with star top half on page 18 along this line.

A2

A1

A3

B2

B1

C2

C1

C3

Star
Bottom Half

Crazy Sand Dollars

Combing the beach for keepsakes is a fun and interesting pastime. Whether at the river, lake, or ocean, it's always fun to be on the lookout. A sand dollar is always a treasured find!

MATERIALS

Yardage is based on 42"-wide fabric.

⅓ yard **each** of 5 assorted blue, brown, taupe, and cream prints for blocks (20 total)*

1⅓ yards of gray floral for outer border

1 yard of tan microdot for block centers and inner border

⅔ yard of dark-brown print for binding

5 yards of fabric for backing

74" x 81" piece of batting

Freezer paper

*If all your fabrics are at least 42" wide, you'll be able to make 80 blocks. However, you only need 72 blocks to make the quilt shown on page 22. So, if a few fabrics aren't 42" wide, you can still use them.

CUTTING

From the tan microdot, cut:
7 strips, 1½" x 42"

From the gray floral, cut:
7 strips, 5½" x 42"

From the dark-brown print, cut:
8 strips, 2½" x 42"

MAKING THE BLOCKS

Before you begin, see "General Craziness" on page 5 for detailed instructions.

1. Stack the 20 blue, brown, taupe, and cream prints in a pile, right sides up. As you stack, align the selvage and left side of each piece. Try to have contrast from one piece to the next, either by print or color. Every four fabrics will be together in the same block. I started with blue on the bottom; then stacked brown, taupe, cream, blue, brown, taupe, cream, blue, and so on, ending with cream on top. Divide the stack into two piles of 10 fabrics each for cutting.

2. Trace the Sand Dollar pattern on pattern sheets 2 and 3 four times side by side onto the uncoated side of a piece of freezer paper, making sure to abut the patterns so the outer lines are touching and there's no space between the blocks. Be sure to trace all lines and to label each piece. Repeat to make two additional freezer-paper patterns (one for the second stack and one extra for stacking). Press a freezer-paper pattern onto the top of each stack of fabric.

3. Using a rotary cutter and ruler, cut each of the four block patterns out of the stack of fabric, cutting through the freezer paper and the entire stack of fabric. Note that the sections are labeled alphabetically. Cutting one block apart at a time, cut the block into sections A through D, first separating the left half of the block into section A/B. Then cut the right side of the block into section C/D. (I say the alphabet backward and count backward to determine the cutting order.) Continue cutting until all the individual pieces have been separated. As you cut out each piece, stack the pieces on its own master so you have four stacks of fabric.

4. Remove the freezer paper from all the pieces. Next you'll shuffle the pieces as detailed below so that each element will be a different fabric.

- For pieces A1, B1, C1, and D1, put the top fabric on the bottom of the stack.

- For pieces A4, A5, B4, and C4, put the top **two** fabrics on the bottom of the stack.

- All of the background pieces (A2, A3, B2, B3, D2, D3, C2, and C3) stay where they started.

Made by Sandi McKell and quilted by Karen Brown.
Finished size: 68½" x 75½" • Block size: 7" x 7"

5. To sew the block back together, join the pieces into four sections (A–D) as described below. Remember to refer to the pattern to make sure you sew the correct edges together and follow the dots for placement between sections.

- **Section A.** Stitch A1 to A2, trying to keep the seam adjacent to piece A4 straight. Add A3 and A4, trying to keep the seams adjacent to A5 straight. Add A5, trying to keep the seam adjacent to section B straight.

- **Section B.** Stitch B1 to B2, trying to keep the seam adjacent to section A straight. Add B3, trying to keep the seam adjacent to B4 straight. Add B4, trying to keep the seam adjacent to section A straight.

- **Section C.** Stitch C1 to C2, trying to keep the seam adjacent to section A straight. Add C3, trying

to keep the seam adjacent to C4 straight. Add C4, trying to keep the seam adjacent to section A straight.

- **Section D.** Stitch D1 to D2, trying to keep the seam adjacent to section B straight. Add D3, trying to keep the seam adjacent to section C straight.

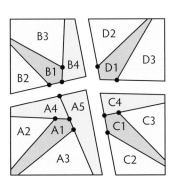

6. Straighten the edges before stitching one section to another section, making sure to only trim the edges you're sewing. Join the sections as follows.
   - **Join A and B,** trying to keep the inside seam adjacent to section D straight.
   - **Join C and D,** trying to keep the inside seam adjacent to section A straight.
   - **Sew A/B to C/D,** centering the right and left sides of the block and making sure that it looks like pieces A1, B1, C1, and D1 would intersect.

7. Repeat to make a total of 80 blocks. Only 72 blocks are needed for this project. Save the remaining blocks for another project or use them to piece a cute backing for your quilt.

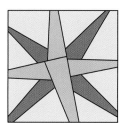

Make 80.

8. Using the circle pattern on pattern sheet 3, appliqué a tan circle in the center of each block.

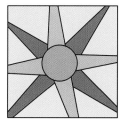

9. Press and square up the blocks to measure 7½" x 7½".

• MAKE IT BIGGER

If you want to make a larger quilt, use the leftover blocks to make 10 rows of nine blocks each. (The quilt will measure 68½" x 82½") For the inner border, cut two 70½"-long strips and two 58½"-long strips. For the outer border, cut two 72½"-long strips and two 68½"-long strips.

ASSEMBLING THE QUILT TOP

1. Lay out the blocks in nine rows of eight blocks each as shown in the quilt assembly diagram. Sew the blocks together in rows. Press the seam allowances in opposite directions from row to row. Join the rows. Press the seam allowances in one direction.

2. For the inner border, join the tan-microdot 1½"-wide strips end to end. From the pieced strip, cut two 63½"-long strips for the side borders and two 58½"-long strips for the top and bottom borders. Sew the side borders to the quilt top first, and then add the top and bottom borders. Press all seam allowances toward the inner border.

3. For the outer border, join the gray-floral 5½"-wide strips end to end. From the pieced strip, cut two 65½"-long strips for the side borders and two 68½"-long strips for the top and bottom borders. Sew the side borders to the quilt top first, and then add the top and bottom borders. Press all seam allowances toward the outer border.

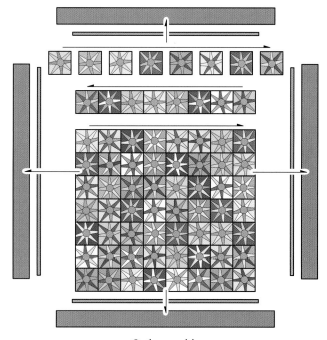

Quilt assembly

FINISHING THE QUILT

If you need help with any of the following finishing tasks, go to ShopMartingale.com/HowtoQuilt for free, downloadable information. Layer the quilt top with batting and backing; baste. Hand or machine quilt as desired. Use the dark-brown 2½"-wide strips to make and attach the binding.

Crazy Summer Blooms

*I love having summer flowers on the table, and
these will always be fresh and stay oh-so pretty!*

MATERIALS

Yardage is based on 42"-wide fabric.

22 rectangles, 16" x 19", of assorted wools for blocks*

½ yard of brown solid for binding

1½ yards of fabric for backing

21" x 102" piece of batting

¾ yard of 16"-wide paper-backed fusible web

Freezer paper

I used a variety of red, orange, berry, plum, gold, turquoise, brown, and tobacco wools, plus one mint green.

CUTTING

From the brown solid, cut:
6 strips, 2½" x 42"

ABOUT WOOL

I used hand-dyed wools that were already felted (washed and dried). If you purchase wool off the bolt, wash the wool in hot water and dry it in the dryer on a normal heat setting.

Often wool doesn't have a right or wrong side. However, with hand-dyed wool, one side can be different than the other side. So, when using hand-dyed wool, you need to pick one side as the "right" side.

When piecing with wool, press the seam allowances open. Use a wool setting on your iron; I use steam even with wool. Some people like to use a walking foot when piecing with wool because the fabric is bulkier than cotton. I've never had a problem, so I don't use a walking foot.

Following my grandma's lead, I use a cotton fabric as the backing on a wool quilt (so I don't itch!). I also used cotton fabric for the binding and a cotton batting.

MAKING THE BLOCKS

Before you begin, see "General Craziness" on page 5 for detailed instructions.

1. Stack the wool rectangles in a pile, right side up and raw edges aligned. Starting with a light fabric on the bottom, stack the rectangles light, dark, light, dark, and so on. Try to have contrast from one fabric to the next. Every two fabrics will be together in the same block. You won't be able to cut through as many wool pieces as you can with cotton, so you need to separate the wool pieces into piles. The number of pieces in each pile will depend on the thickness of the wool and the size of your rotary cutter. Start with four to six pieces in each pile and adjust as necessary for your circumstances.

PLAN AHEAD — — · —

After cutting, the individual pieces (such as A1) will be combined into one stack of 22 pieces. When you separate the layers into multiple stacks, keep track of the order so you can cut the bottom fabrics first. That way, when you stack them on the master, they will be on the bottom. You'll continue cutting your way up through your stack of 22 fabrics and stacking them on the master, making sure to keep all the fabrics in order.

2. Trace the Flower pattern on pattern sheet 4 onto the uncoated side of a piece of freezer paper. Be sure to trace all lines and to label each piece. You'll need a freezer-paper pattern for each stack of wool; the number you'll need depends on how many stacks of wool you have. Press a freezer-paper pattern onto the top of each stack of wool.

3. Cut the square out of each stack, cutting through the freezer paper and the entire stack of wool. Separate the A/B half of the block from the C/D half of the block. Cut the pattern apart into sections A through D. (I say the alphabet backward and count backward to determine the cutting order.) Continue cutting until all the individual pieces have been separated. As you cut out each piece, stack the pieces on the master so you have one stack of fabrics.

4. Remove the freezer paper from all the pieces. Next, shuffle the stack so that the flower will be one fabric and the background will be another fabric. For pieces A1, B1, C1, and D1, put the top fabric on the bottom of each of the piles. You now have a two-colored block!

5. To sew the blocks back together, join the pieces into four sections (A–D) as described below. Refer to the pattern to make sure you sew the correct edges together and follow the dots for placement between sections. Press the seam allowances open after sewing each seam.

   Sections A, B, C, and D. Center piece 2 on top of piece 1 and stitch. Straighten the edges if necessary before adding pieces 3 and 4, keeping the inside edges of the block straight.

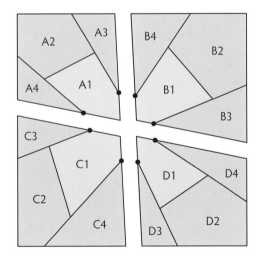

6. Straighten the edges before stitching one section to another, making sure to only trim the edges you're sewing. Join the sections as follows.

- **Join section A to section B,** matching the flower seams.

- **Join section C to section D,** matching the flower seams.

- **Sew A/B to C/D,** centering C/D on top of A/B. The seam intersections won't necessarily match.

Made by Sandi McKell and quilted by Karen Brown.

Finished size: 18½" x 99½" • *Block size:* 9" x 9"

7. Repeat to make a total of 22 blocks.

Make 22.

8. Referring to "Fusible Wool Appliqué" on page 11 and using the patterns below, cut out the flower centers from the assorted wools. Using matching thread and a whipstitch, appliqué a flower center in the center of each block as shown in the photo on page 26.

9. Press and square up the blocks to measure 9½" x 9½".

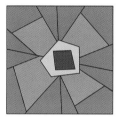

ASSEMBLING THE TABLE RUNNER

Lay out the blocks in two rows of 11 blocks each as shown in the table-runner assembly diagram. Sew the blocks together in rows and press the seam allowances open. Join the rows and press the seam allowances open.

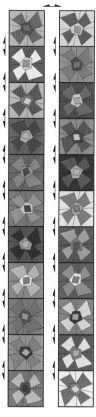

Table-runner assembly

FINISHING THE TABLE RUNNER

If you need help with any of the following finishing tasks, go to ShopMartingale.com/HowtoQuilt for free, downloadable information. Layer the table-runner top with batting and backing; baste. Hand or machine quilt as desired. Use the brown 2½"-wide strips to make and attach the binding.

Appliqué patterns do not include seam allowances.

Flower center
Make 22 of each.

Crazy Hot

Can't you just feel the heat? I think I need my sunscreen! Even when it's the dead of winter, this quilt will shine with summer's warmth.

MATERIALS

Yardage is based on 42"-wide fabric.

⅞ yard **each** of 7 assorted red, 7 assorted gold, 7 assorted orange, and 7 assorted blue prints or plaids for blocks (28 total)

1⅞ yards of blue stripe for outer border

½ yard of brown print for inner border

¾ yards of dark-blue print for binding

5 yards of fabric for backing

86" x 86" piece of batting

Freezer paper

CUTTING

From *each* of the assorted red, gold, orange and blue prints, cut:

1 square, 27" x 27" (28 total)

From the brown print, cut:

7 strips, 2" x 42"

From the blue stripe, cut:

9 strips, 6½" x 42"

From the dark-blue print for binding, cut:

9 strips, 2½" x 42"

MAKING THE BLOCKS

Before you begin, see "General Craziness" on page 5 for detailed instructions.

1. Stack seven red squares in a pile, right side up. Repeat to make a second pile of seven blue squares. Make a third pile of seven orange squares and a fourth pile of seven gold squares. All of the fabrics in *each* pile must be right side up. As you stack, align the bottom and left side of each square.

PLAN AHEAD

Typically with Crazy blocks it's difficult to predict which fabrics will end up together in the same block, but in this block it's easier! So if you'd like to control your fabric choices, the bottom fabrics of each pile will be together in one of four blocks. Then the next layer of red, blue, orange, and gold (all those fabrics second from the bottom) will be together in one of four blocks. So look at each layer as you stack them to make sure you like your combination of fabrics. Additionally, every two fabrics in each stack will be together as sun points in a block, so there needs to be good contrast between the fabrics.

2. A complete block is made up of four Crazy sun quadrants. Trace the sun-quadrant pattern on pattern sheet 3 four times onto the uncoated side of a piece of freezer paper, placing the patterns side by side with no space between the patterns and rotating the patterns to make a full Sun block. (You can press two pieces of freezer paper together so that the freezer paper is big enough to trace the full sun pattern.) Repeat to make a total of eight full sun patterns (one for each stack of fabric plus four extra to stack on). Press a full sun pattern onto the top of each stack of squares.

3. Using a rotary cutter and ruler, cut the stack, cutting through the freezer paper and the entire stack of fabric. Cut the Sun block into the four quadrants. Cut and piece each quadrant before proceeding to the next quadrant. Start by cutting off section H. Next, cut the top half of the block (A/B/C) from the bottom half (D/E/F/G). Then cut

Pieced by Sandi McKell and quilted by Kathy Woods.
Finished size: 80½" x 80½" • *Block size: 13" x 13"*

the pattern apart into sections A through G. (I say the alphabet backward and count backward to determine the cutting order.) Continue cutting until all the individual pieces have been separated. As you cut out each piece, stack each color on its master so you still have four stacks of fabric, each a different color.

4. Remove the freezer paper from all the pieces. Trade the pattern pieces among the stacks as detailed below until each stack of fabric has a colored sun with a contrasting background.

- Put the red ray pieces (A1, B1, C3, D1, E1, F1, and G1) in the blue stack. Put the blue ray pieces in the orange stack. Put the orange ray pieces in the gold stack. Put the gold ray pieces in the red stack.

- Put the red circle pieces (B2, C2, E2, and F2) in the orange stack. Put the orange circle pieces in the red stack. Put the blue circle pieces in the gold stack and the gold circle pieces the blue stack.

- Put the red center pieces (C1 and H) in the gold stack. Put the gold center pieces in the orange stack. Put the orange center pieces in the blue stack and the blue center pieces in the red stack.

- All of the background pieces (A2, A3, A4, D2, D3, D4, G2, G3, and G4) stay where they started.

 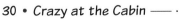

5. Next you'll shuffle the ray pieces so that there will be two different fabrics for the rays. For pieces A1, D1, and G1, put the top fabric on the bottom of each pile. The rays will now be two different fabrics in the same color family.

6. To sew the block back together, join the pieces into seven sections (A–G) as described below. Refer to the pattern to make sure you sew the correct edges together and follow the dots for placement between sections.

- **Section A.** Stitch A1 to A2, trying to keep the seam adjacent to A4 straight. Straighten the edge before adding A3. Add A3, trying to keep the seam adjacent to A4 straight. Center A4 on top of A1/A2/A3 and stitch.

- **Section B.** Stitch B1 to B2, trying to keep the edge adjacent to section A straight.

- **Section C.** Stitch C1 to C2, trying to keep the edge adjacent to C3 straight. Center C3 on top of C1/C2 and stitch.

- **Section D.** Stitch D1 to D2, trying to keep the edge adjacent to D4 straight. Straighten the edge before adding D3. Add D3, trying to keep the edge adjacent to D4 straight. Center D4 on top of D1/D2/D3 and stitch.

- **Section E.** Stitch E1 to E2, trying to keep the edge adjacent to section D straight.

- **Section F.** Center F2 on top of F1 and stitch.

- **Section G.** Stitch G1 to G2, trying to keep the edge adjacent to G4 straight. Straighten the edge before adding G3. Add G3, trying to keep the edge adjacent to G4 straight. Add G4, centering it on top of G1/G2/G3.

7. Straighten the edges before stitching one section to another section, making sure to only trim the edges you're sewing. When you straighten the edges, it's important that the portion you trim off is parallel to your ruler so you don't change the angles of the pattern. Join the sections as follows.

- **Trim both A4 edges.** Join A and B, keeping the edge adjacent to C straight. Trim A/B, making sure you have a ¼" seam allowance at B2.

- **Add C to AB,** matching the seam intersection for the circle at B2 and C2.

- **Trim both D4 edges.** Join D to E, keeping the edge adjacent to F straight. Trim D/E, making sure you have a ¼" seam allowance at E2.

- **Add F to DE,** matching the seam intersection for the circle at E2 and F2.

- **Trim both G4 edges.** Add G to D/E/F, keeping the edge adjacent to C straight.

- **Trim A/B/C,** making sure you have a ¼" seam allowance at C2. Join A/B/C to D/E/F/G, matching the seam intersection for the circle at F2 and C2.

- **Add H,** centering the edge of H on the inner circle (B2, C1, C2, E2, and F2).

8. Repeat to make four matching quadrants for one block.

9. Trim the two inside edges of each quadrant as shown, positioning a ruler so that the seams for the inner circle (B2 and E2) are 2¾" from the upper-right corner. The points of the rays (B1 and E1) should be about 7" from the corner on the ruler, which gives you a ¼" seam allowance along the edge of the block after trimming. Your blocks may be larger or smaller, but pick consistent numbers for each set of four quadrants. For the circle to appear round and the points to match, it's important to use a consistent measurement for each set of four quadrants.

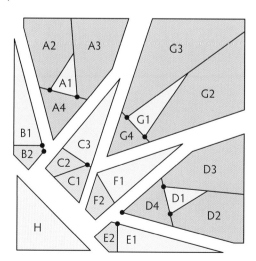

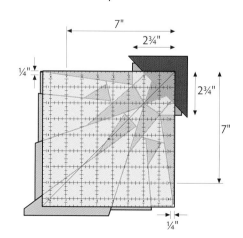

10. Join the quadrants from step 9, matching the center seam intersections and the seams for the inner circle. Try to match the sun points (B1 and E1), but don't worry if they don't match exactly.

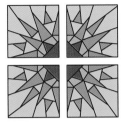 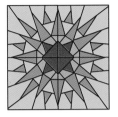

11. Press and square up the block to measure 13½" x 13½".

12. Repeat to make a total of 27 blocks. Only 25 blocks are required for this project. Save the remaining blocks for another project, such as "Welcome to the Lake" on page 61, or use them to piece a cute back for your quilt.

ASSEMBLING THE QUILT TOP

1. Lay out the blocks in five rows of five blocks each as shown in the quilt assembly diagram below. Sew the blocks together in rows. Press the seam allowances in opposite directions from row to row. Join the rows. Press the seam allowances in one direction.

2. For the inner border, join the brown 2"-wide strips end to end. From the pieced strip, cut two 65½"-long strips for the side borders and two 68½"-long strips for the top and bottom borders. Sew the side borders to the quilt top first, and then add the top and bottom borders. Press all seam allowances toward the inner border.

3. For the outer border, join the blue-striped 6½"-wide strips end to end. From the pieced strip, cut four 89"-long strips. Sew the outer borders to the quilt top and miter the corners, referring to ShopMartingale.com/extras as needed for free, downloadable instructions. Press all seam allowances toward the outer border.

FINISHING THE QUILT

If you need help with any of the following finishing tasks, go to ShopMartingale.com/HowtoQuilt for free, downloadable information. Layer the quilt top with batting and backing; baste. Hand or machine quilt as desired. Use the dark-blue 2½"-wide strips to make and attach the binding.

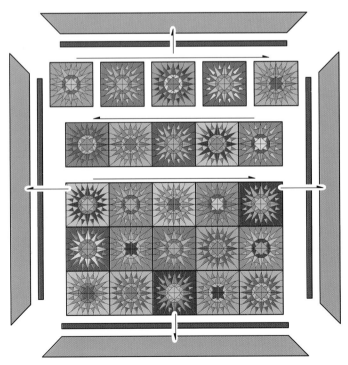

Quilt assembly

What a Hoot!

We have owls that hang out in our big old trees that were planted when our property was homesteaded in the late 1800s. As my friend Sandi was piecing these owls for me, she shared a saying her dad used to tell her, and I knew it needed be part of this quilt! Isn't it just perfect?

MATERIALS

Yardage is based on 42"-wide fabric. Fat quarters measure 18" x 21" and fat eighths measure 9" x 21".

1 fat quarter **each** of 3 assorted gold, 3 assorted red, 3 assorted dark-brown, and 2 assorted tan or multicolored prints or plaids for Owl blocks and sashing strips (11 total)

¾ yard of tan-and-red plaid for Owl blocks and sashing strips

11 fat quarters of assorted green prints for Star blocks and leaf appliqués

¾ yard of medium-brown plaid for tree trunk

⅙ yard of brown paisley for branch #1

⅙ yard of light-brown stripe for branch #2

¼ yard of dark-brown stripe for branch #3

1 fat eighth of brown-and-black plaid for branch #4

⅓ yard of brown word print for branch #5

½ yard of rust-and-brown plaid for background #1

⅝ yard of rust stripe for background #2

⅝ yard of rust plaid for background #3

1 fat eighth of red-and-tan check for background #4

½ yard of tobacco print for background #5

⅝ yard of caramel plaid for background #6

½ yard of caramel stripe for background #7

⅝ yard of caramel-and-cream stripe for background #8

⅝ yard of caramel print for background #9

1 fat eighth of caramel-and-tan check for background #10

1 fat eighth of caramel-and-tan plaid for background #11

⅛ yard **total** of assorted gold prints for owl beaks

⅓ yard of green plaid for top border

½ yard of 42"-wide brown-and-black houndstooth wool for letters

14" x 16" rectangle of green wool for owl outer eyes

7" x 16" rectangle of yellow wool for owl inner eyes

6" x 7" rectangle of black or dark-green wool for owl pupils

¾ yard of brown print for binding

5¼ yards of fabric for backing

72" x 89" piece of batting

2½ yards of 16"-wide paper-backed fusible web

Freezer paper

The wise old owl lived in an oak

The more he saw the less he spoke

The less he spoke the more he heard

Why can't we be like that old bird?

Pieced by Sandi McKell and Janet Nesbitt and quilted by Karen Brown.

Finished size: 66½" x 83½" • Owl block size: 8½" x 8½" • Star block size: 6" x 6"

CUTTING

From background #1, cut:
1 rectangle, 6½" x 8"
1 rectangle, 6½" x 9"
1 rectangle, 5½" x 9"
1 rectangle, 5" x 7½"
1 rectangle, 3½" x 6"
1 rectangle, 3½" x 4½"
1 rectangle, 3" x 4½"
2 rectangles, 2½" x 9"
1 rectangle, 2½" x 4½"

1 rectangle, 2" x 12½"
2 rectangles 2" x 9"
3 squares, 2" x 2"
1 rectangle, 1½" x 10"
1 rectangle, 1½" x 8"
1 rectangle, 1½" x 2½"
6 squares, 1½" x 1½"
3 squares, 1" x 1"

Continued on page 36

Continued from page 35

From background #2, cut:
1 rectangle, 10½" x 11½"
1 rectangle, 7" x 16"
1 rectangle, 5½" x 7"
1 rectangle, 5½" x 11½"
1 rectangle, 3½" x 13½"
1 rectangle, 2½" x 12½"
1 rectangle, 2½" x 4"
1 square, 2" x 2"
1 rectangle, 1½" x 9"
1 rectangle, 1½" x 4"
1 rectangle, 1" x 1½"
1 square, 1½" x 1½"
1 square, 1" x 1"

From background #3, cut:
1 rectangle, 5" x 10½"
1 rectangle, 7½" x 9½"
1 rectangle, 16½" x 18½"

From background #4, cut:
1 rectangle, 2½" x 5"
1 rectangle, 1½" x 2½"
3 squares, 1½" x 1½"

From background #5, cut:
1 rectangle, 8" x 11½"
1 rectangle, 7½" x 9½"
1 square, 6½" x 6½"
1 rectangle, 5½" x 9½"
1 square, 4½" x 4½"
1 rectangle, 4" x 9"
1 rectangle, 3½" x 7½"
1 rectangle, 3" x 4"
1 square, 3" x 3"
1 square, 2½" x 2½"
1 rectangle, 2" x 12"
1 rectangle, 1½" x 5½"
2 squares, 1½" x 1½"

From background #6, cut:
1 rectangle, 10" x 18½"
1 rectangle, 8½" x 22"
1 rectangle, 3½" x 11"
1 rectangle, 2½" x 7"
1 rectangle, 1½" x 6½"
2 squares, 1½" x 1½"

From background #7, cut:
1 rectangle, 6½" x 25½"
1 rectangle, 6½" x 7½"
1 square, 6½" x 6½"
1 rectangle, 5½" x 16½"
2 squares, 5½" x 5½"
1 rectangle, 3½" x 5½"
1 rectangle, 2" x 9"
1 rectangle, 1½" x 9½"
1 square, 1½" x 1½"

From background #8, cut:
1 rectangle, 11½" x 15½"
1 rectangle, 9½" x 18½"
1 rectangle, 5" x 8½"
1 rectangle, 1" x 3½"
1 square, 1" x 1"

From background #9, cut:
1 rectangle, 14½" x 17½"
1 rectangle, 6" x 9½"
1 square, 4½" x 4½"
1 rectangle, 3" x 4½"
1 rectangle, 3½" x 7½"
1 square, 3½" x 3½"
1 rectangle, 2½" x 3½"
1 rectangle, 2" x 2½"
2 squares, 2½" x 2½"
1 rectangle, 2" x 9½"
1 rectangle, 1" x 8½"
1 rectangle, 1" x 1½"
1 square, 1" x 1"

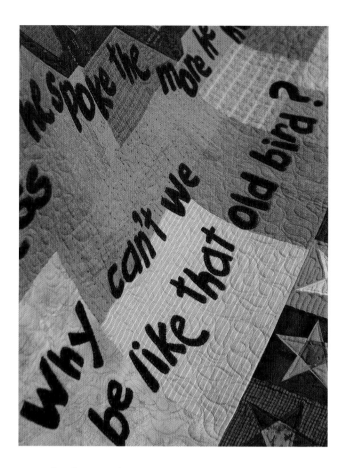

From background #10, cut:
1 rectangle, 2½" x 4½"
2 rectangles, 2½" x 4"
1 rectangle, 3½" x 4½"
3 squares, 1½" x 1½"
1 square, 1" x 1"

From background #11, cut:
1 rectangle, 2½" x 7"
1 square, 2½" x 2½"
1 rectangle, 2" x 9"

From 1 of the tan or multicolored plaid fat quarters for Owl 1, cut:*
1 rectangle, 3½" x 10½"
1 rectangle, 2" x 9"
1 square, 1½" x 1½"

From the dark-brown plaid fat quarter for Owl 4, cut:*
1 rectangle, 2" x 9"
1 square, 2" x 2"

From the tan-and-red plaid for Owl 8, cut:*
1 rectangle, 18" x 21"
1 rectangle, 5½" x 21½"
1 square, 5" x 5"
1 rectangle, 2½" x 9"
1 rectangle, 1½" x 9"
1 rectangle, 1½" x 2½"

From 1 of the red print fat quarters for Owl 11, cut:*
1 rectangle, 5½" x 10"
1 square, 4½" x 4½"
1 rectangle, 1½" x 9"

From the medium-brown plaid for Tree Trunk, cut:
1 rectangle, 9½" x 14½"
1 rectangle, 7½" x 15"
1 rectangle, 6½" x 13"
1 rectangle, 5½" x 10½"
2 rectangles, 5½" x 7½"
1 square, 5" x 5"
1 rectangle, 4½" x 17½"
1 square, 4½" x 4½"
1 rectangle, 2½" x 3½"
1 square, 2½" x 2½"
1 square, 1½" x 1½"

From the brown paisley for Branch 1, cut:
1 rectangle, 3½" x 4½"
1 rectangle, 2½" x 3½"
1 rectangle, 2½" x 4½"
1 rectangle, 2" x 4½"
1 rectangle, 2" x 3½"
1 square, 2" x 2"
1 rectangle, 1½" x 7½"
1 square, 1½" x 1½"

From the light-brown stripe for Branch 2, cut:
1 rectangle, 3½" x 4½"
1 rectangle, 2½" x 3½"
1 rectangle, 2½" x 4½"
1 rectangle, 2½" x 5½"
1 rectangle, 2" x 2½"
1 rectangle, 2" x 3½"

From the dark-brown stripe for Branch 3, cut:
1 rectangle, 6½" x 7"
1 rectangle, 5½" x 6½"
1 square, 2½" x 2½"
1 rectangle, 2" x 12½"
1 rectangle, 2" x 8½"
1 rectangle, 2" x 3½"
1 rectangle, 1½" x 3"
1 square, 1½" x 1½"

*Wait to cut the pieces listed until after the Owl blocks have been cut out.

Continued on page 38

Continued from page 37

From the brown-and-black plaid for Branch 4, cut:
1 rectangle, 3½" x 7½"
1 rectangle, 2½" x 3½"
1 rectangle, 2½" x 3"
1 rectangle, 2½" x 9"
1 square, 2½" x 2½"
1 rectangle, 1½" x 3"
1 rectangle, 1½" x 2½"
1 rectangle, 1" x 1½"
1 square, 1½" x 1½"

From the brown word print for Branch 5, cut:
1 rectangle, 6½" x 8½"
1 rectangle, 4½" x 6"
1 rectangle, 3½" x 5½"
1 rectangle, 2½" x 4½"
1 rectangle, 3½" x 5"
1 rectangle, 2½" x 3½"
2 rectangles, 3" x 3½"
1 rectangle, 2½" x 6½"
1 rectangle, 2½" x 8½"
1 rectangle, 2" x 2½"
1 rectangle, 2" x 4"
1 rectangle, 1½" x 8½"
2 squares, 1½" x 1½"

From the green plaid for top border, cut:
2 strips, 4½" x 42"

From the brown print for binding, cut:
8 strips, 2½" x 42"

MAKING THE OWL BLOCKS

Before you begin, see "General Craziness" on page 5 for detailed instructions.

1. Stack the 11 fat quarters for the Owl blocks and the tan-and-red plaid 18" x 21" rectangle (12 total pieces) in a pile, right side up. As you stack, align the selvage and left side of each fat quarter. Try to have contrast from one piece to the next, either by print or color. Every three fabrics will be together in the same block. I started with gold on the bottom; then stacked red, tan, brown, gold, red, tan, brown, and so on, ending with brown on top.

2. Trace the owl pattern on pattern sheet 2 onto the uncoated side of a piece of freezer paper. Be sure to trace all the lines and to label each section. Press the freezer-paper template onto the top of the stack of fat quarters.

3. Using a rotary cutter and ruler, cut the rectangle from the stack of fabric, cutting through the freezer paper and the entire stack of fabric. Note that the sections are labeled alphabetically. Start by cutting both wing sections (E/F and G/H) from the body section (A/B/C/D). Then cut the pattern apart into sections A through H. (I say the alphabet backward and count backward to determine the cutting order.) Continue cutting until all the individual pieces have been separated. As you cut out each piece, stack the pieces on the master pattern to stay organized.

4. Remove the freezer paper from all the pieces. Next you'll shuffle the pattern pieces so each element will be a different fabric.

   • For owl stomach piece A4, put the top fabric on the bottom of the stack.

   • For owl body pieces A2, A3, B1, B5, B6, C1, D1, E1, F1, G1, and H1, put the top *two* fabrics on the bottom of the stack.

   • Background pieces B2, B3, B4, C2, D2, E2, E3, F2, F3, G2, G3, H2, and H3 will stay where they started.

5. For the beaks, press the A1 freezer-paper pattern onto the right side of the gold fabric and cut around the paper template. Cut out 12 beaks. If cutting more than one at a time, make sure all of the fabric is right side up. Discard the beaks cut from the fat quarters and add the gold beaks to your stack.

6. To sew the block back together, join the pieces into eight sections (A–H) as describe below. Refer to the pattern to make sure you sew the correct edges together and follow the dots for placement between sections.

- **Section A.** Center A2 on top of A1 and stitch. Add A3, making sure there is extra fabric at the beak's point. Before adding A4, straighten the edge as needed. Center A4 on top of A1/A2/A3 and stitch.

- **Section B.** Center and stitch B1 to B2. Before adding B3, straighten the edge. Center and stitch B3. Before adding B4, straighten the edge. Add B4, keeping the seam adjacent to B5 straight. Add B5, keeping the seam adjacent to B6 straight. Add B6, keeping the seam adjacent to section A straight.

- **Section C.** Stitch C1 to C2, keeping the seam adjacent to section F straight.

- **Section D.** Stitch D1 to D2, keeping the seam adjacent to section H straight.

- **Section E.** Stitch E1 to E2, keeping the seam adjacent to E3 straight. Add E3, keeping the seam adjacent to section C straight.

- **Section F.** Stitch F1 to F2, keeping the seam adjacent to F3 straight. Add F3, keeping the seam adjacent to section C straight.

- **Section G.** Stitch G1 to G2, keeping the seam adjacent to G3 straight. Add G3, keeping the seam adjacent to section D straight.

- **Section H.** Stitch H1 to H2, keeping the seam adjacent to H3 straight. Add H3, keeping the seam adjacent to section D straight.

7. Straighten the edges before stitching one section to another section, making sure to only trim the edges you're sewing. Join the sections as follows.

- **Center A on B and stitch.**
- **Add C to A/B,** trying to keep the bottom of the block straight.
- Prior to adding section D to A/B/C, trim piece D1 along the base of the block. **Add D to A/B/C,** trying to keep the bottom of the block straight.
- **Join E and F.**
- **Add E/F to A/B/C,** centering the sections.
- **Join G and H.**
- **Add G/H to A/B/D,** centering the sections.

8. Repeat to make 12 Owl blocks. Only 11 blocks are needed for this project. Save the remaining block for another project or use it to make a label for the back of the quilt.

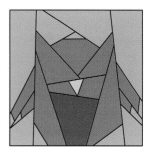

Make 12.

9. Referring to "Fusible Wool Appliqué" on page 11 and using the patterns on page 46, cut out 22 green wool outer-eye pieces, 22 yellow wool inner-eye pieces, and 22 black/dark-green wool pupils. Layer an inner eye on top of an outer eye, and then place a pupil on top of the inner eye. Position the pupils on each owl differently so that the owls appear to be looking in different directions. Whipstitch the eyes in place.

10. Press and square up the blocks to measure 9" x 9".

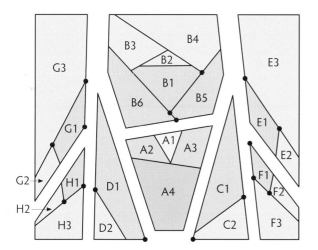

MAKING THE STAR BLOCKS

Before you begin, see "General Craziness" on page 5 for detailed instructions.

1. Stack the 11 green fat quarters in a pile, right side up. As you stack, align the selvage edge and left side of each piece. Try to have contrast from one piece to the next, either by print or color. Every two fabrics will be together in the same block.

2. Trace the star pattern on pages 18 and 19 onto the uncoated side of a piece of freezer paper. Be sure to trace all the lines and to label each section. Press the freezer-paper pattern to the top of the stack of fat quarters.

3. Using a rotary cutter and ruler, cut the block out of the stack of fat quarters, cutting through the freezer paper and the entire stack of fabric. Note that the sections are labeled alphabetically. Start cutting at the letter closest to the end of the alphabet and work backward until you get to A. (I say the alphabet backward and count backward to determine the cutting order.) Continue cutting until all the individual pieces have been separated. As you cut out each piece, stack the pieces on the master pattern to stay organized.

4. Remove the freezer paper from all the pieces. Next you'll shuffle the pattern pieces among the stack as detailed below so that each element is a different fabric.

   - For star-point pieces A2, A3, B1, C1, and D1, put the top fabric on the bottom of the stack.

   - For star-center piece A1, put the top **two** fabrics on the bottom of the stack.

   - All the background pieces (B2, C2, C3, D2, and D3) stay where they started.

5. To sew the block back together, join the pieces into four sections (A–D) as described below. Refer to the pattern to make sure you sew the correct edges together and follow the dots for placement between sections.

   - **Section A.** Center A2 on top of A1 and stitch. Center A3 on top of A1/A2 and stitch.

   - **Section B.** Stitch B1 to B2, keeping the seam adjacent to section A straight (noted by dot on pattern).

   - **Section C.** Stitch piece C1 to C2, and then add C3, trying to keep the inside seam adjacent to section A straight (noted by dot on pattern). Straighten the C1/C2 edge before adding C3.

- **Section D.** Stitch D1 to D2, and then add D3, trying to keep the inside seam adjacent to section A straight (noted by dot on pattern). Straighten the D1/D2 edge before adding D3.

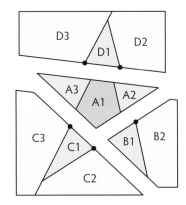

6. Straighten the edges before stitching one section to another section, making sure to only trim the edges you're sewing. Join the sections as follows.

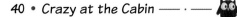

- **Join A to B,** matching the star-point seams.
- **Add C to A/B,** centering the edge of C1 with A1. The seam intersections probably won't match up.
- **Add D to A/B/C,** centering D1 with A1. Again, the seam intersections probably won't match up.

7. Press and square up the block to measure 6½" x 6½", centering the star.

8. Repeat to make a total of 11 blocks.

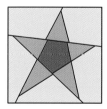

Make 11.

ASSEMBLING THE QUILT TOP

Refer to the photo on page 35 and the assembly diagram on page 46 for placement guidance throughout.

1. Before sewing, lay out the pieces for each section as shown in the diagrams on pages 42–45. Note that most sections require sew-and-flip corners, or what I call geese units. To make the geese units, place an appropriately sized square on the corner of the required rectangle or square. Stitch diagonally from corner to corner. Trim the outside corner of the small square **only,** ¼" from the stitched line. Press the resulting triangle open.

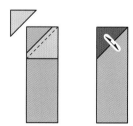

2. Join the Owl blocks and appropriate pieces to make sections 1–5 and sections 7–10. Press the seam allowances in one direction. (In most cases, I press the seam allowances toward the piece with the fewest seams.)

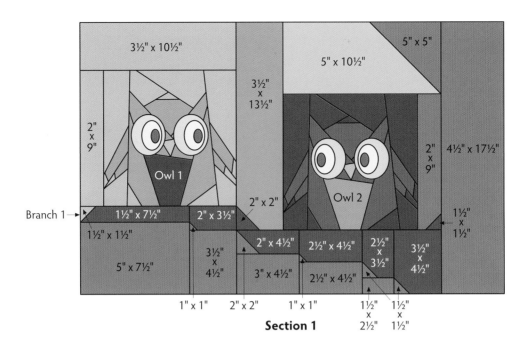

Section 1

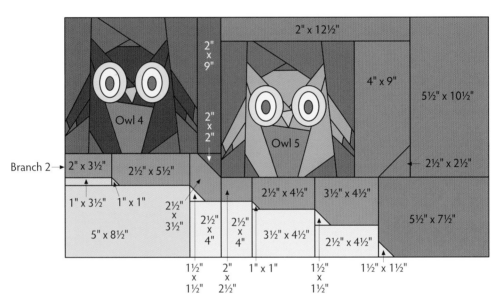

Section 2

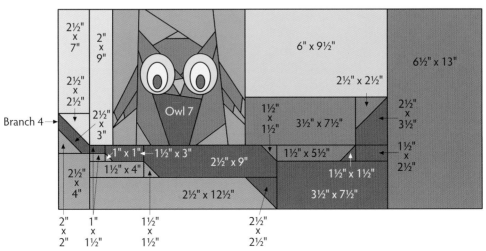

Section 3

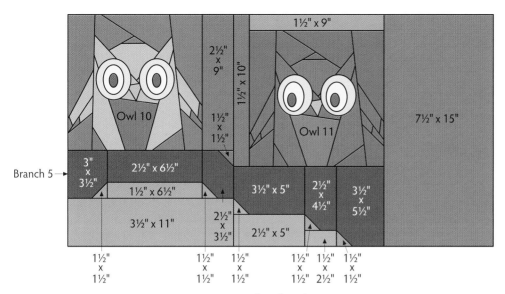

Section 4

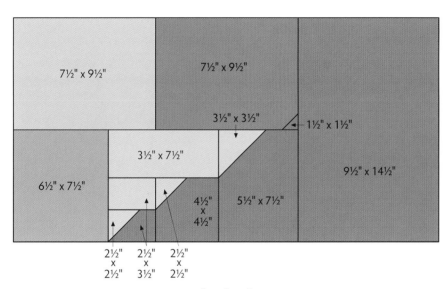

Section 5

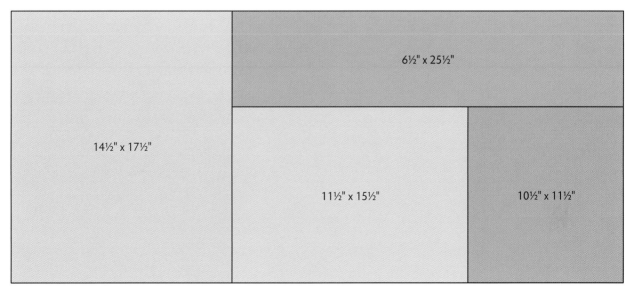

Section 10

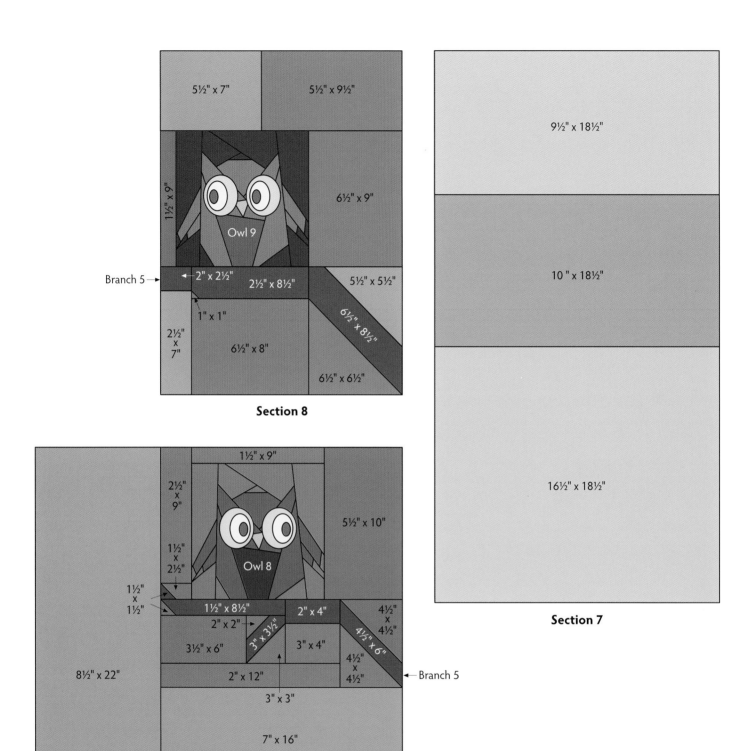

Section 8

5½" x 7"

5½" x 9½"

1½" x 9"

Owl 9

6½" x 9"

Branch 5 →

2" x 2½"

2½" x 8½"

5½" x 5½"

1" x 1"

6½" x 8½"

2½" x 7"

6½" x 8"

6½" x 6½"

Section 7

9½" x 18½"

10 " x 18½"

16½" x 18½"

Section 9

1½" x 9"

2½" x 9"

5½" x 10"

1½" x 2½"

Owl 8

1½" x 1½"

1½" x 8½"

2" x 4"

4½" x 4½"

2" x 2"

3" x 3½"

4½" x 6"

3½" x 6"

3" x 4"

4½" x 4½"

8½" x 22"

2" x 12"

← Branch 5

3" x 3"

7" x 16"

3. For section 6, join the Owl blocks and appropriate pieces to make four units. Then stitch the units together using a partial seam. Referring to the diagram and using partial seams, sew the Owl-block unit to the caramel 3" x 4½" rectangle. Add the upper-left unit, and then the upper-right unit. Then add the lower-right unit. Complete the partial seam to make section 6. Press the seam allowances as indicated.

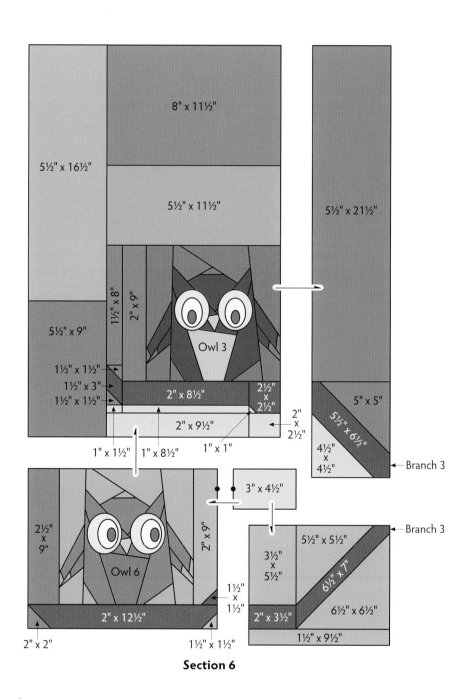

Section 6

4. Sew the sections together as shown in the quilt assembly diagram below.

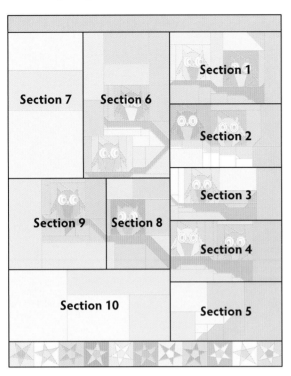

Quilt assembly

5. Join the Star blocks to make a border strip. Sew the strip to the bottom of the quilt top. Press the seam allowances toward the quilt center.

6. Join the green-plaid 4½"-wide strips end to end. From the pieced strip, cut a 66½"-long strip. Sew the strip to the top of the quilt top. Press the seam allowances toward the green-plaid strip.

7. Using the leaf patterns on page 47, make eight small green leaves and six large green leaves. Appliqué the small leaves to the ends of the branches using needle-turn appliqué or your favorite method. Appliqué the large leaves across the top of the quilt top as shown in the photo on page 35. Refer to ShopMartingale.com/HowtoQuilt for free, downloadable appliqué instructions.

8. Referring to "Fusible Wool Appliqué" on page 11 and using the letter patterns on pages 48–49, cut out the words from the brown wool. Using matching thread, whipstitch the letters in place.

FINISHING THE QUILT

If you need help with any of the following finishing tasks, go to ShopMartingale.com/HowtoQuilt for free, downloadable information. Layer the quilt top with batting and backing; baste. Hand or machine quilt as desired. Use the brown 2½"-wide strips to make and attach the binding.

Patterns do not include seam allowances. Add seam allowance for needle-turn appliqué

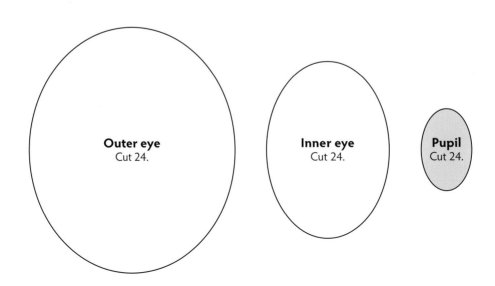

Outer eye
Cut 24.

Inner eye
Cut 24.

Pupil
Cut 24.

Appliqué patterns do not include seam allowances.

Some letters in this section are used in Crazy Moose Messages on page 71.

Large leaf
Cut 6.

Patterns do not include seam allowances. Add seam allowance for needle-turn appliqué

Small leaf
Cut 8.

Cut 3.

Cut 12.

Cut 4.

Cut 5.

Cut 1.

Cut 12.

Cut 5.

Cut 7.

Cut 8.

Appliqué patterns do not include seam allowances.

Cut 3.

Cut 8.

Cut 1.

Cut 2.

Cut 6.

Cut 9.

Cut 2.

Cut 4.

Cut 5.

Cut 2.

Cut 1.

Cut 4.

Cut 5.

Cut 1.

Cut 1.

Cut 1.

Cut 1.

Cut 1.

Appliqué patterns do not include seam allowances.

Crazy Regatta

I fell in love with boat parades when we lived in California, and especially enjoyed the parade of decorated boats at Christmastime. The fun continues every summer at the lake with the Fourth of July boat parade. Deep down, everybody loves a parade!

MATERIALS

Yardage is based on 42"-wide fabric. Fat quarters measure 18" x 21".

7 fat quarters of assorted prints (2 navy blue, 1 light blue, 1 red, 1 gold, 1 green, and 1 cream) for Sailboat blocks

6 fat quarters of assorted prints (1 dark brown, 1 green, 1 caramel, 1 red, 1 yellow, and 1 cream) for Houseboat blocks

6 fat quarters of assorted prints (1 blue, 1 red, 1 yellow, 1 green, 1 navy, and 1 cream) for Motorboat blocks

6 fat quarters of assorted prints (2 blue, 1 red, 1 yellow, 1 dark brown, and 1 tan) for Party Barge blocks

10 fat quarters of assorted dark-blue and dark-green prints for Wave blocks and scrappy binding*

10 fat quarters of assorted light-aqua prints for Wave blocks*

4" x 4" square of gold wool for the moon on the Houseboat blocks

6" x 6" square of green wool for palm-tree leaves on Party Barge blocks

2" x 5" rectangle of brown wool for palm-tree trunk on Party Barge blocks

3 yards of fabric for backing

51" x 66" piece of batting

1¼ yards of ½"-long teal pom-poms for roof on Party Barge blocks

¼ yard of 16"-wide paper-backed fusible web

Freezer paper

Embroidery floss (optional)

Permanent pen (optional)

Each of the light-aqua prints needs to contrast with each of the dark-blue and green prints. If you're planning to make "Welcome to the Lake" on page 61, select 12 light and 12 dark fat quarters for the Wave blocks and make them all at once!

CUTTING

After cutting out the Crazy blocks, cut the following pieces.

From *each* of the Motorboat fat quarters, cut:
   1 rectangle, 2½" x 9½" (6 total)

From *each* of the Party Barge fat quarters, cut:
   1 rectangle, 3½" x 9½" (6 total)

From the assorted dark-blue and dark-green prints, cut a *total* of:
   11 strips, 2½" x 21"

Pieced by Sandi McKell and quilted by Kathy Woods.

Finished size: 45½" x 60½" • Boat block size: 9" x 9" • Wave block size: 3" x 3"

MAKING THE SAILBOAT BLOCKS

Before you begin, see "General Craziness" on page 5 for detailed instructions.

1. Stack the seven fat quarters for the sailboats in a pile, right side up. As you stack, align the selvage and left side of each fat quarter. Every four fabrics will be together in the same block. Starting on the bottom, you can think: boat and pennant, followed by mast and boat stripe, sail, and then the fourth fabric in each block is the background.

2. Trace the sailboat pattern on pattern sheet 4 onto the uncoated side of the freezer paper. Be sure to trace all lines and to label each section. Press the freezer-paper pattern onto the stack of fat quarters.

3. Using a rotary cutter and ruler, cut the block from the stack, cutting through the freezer paper and the entire stack of fabric. Note that the sections are labeled alphabetically. Start cutting at the letter closest to the end of the alphabet and work backward until you get to A. (I say the alphabet backward and count backward to determine the cutting order.) Continue cutting until all the individual pieces have been separated. As you cut out each piece, stack the pieces on the master to stay organized.

4. Remove the freezer paper from all the pieces. Next you'll shuffle the pattern pieces as detailed below so that each element will be a different fabric.

- For the sail (A1 and B1), put the top fabric on the bottom of the pile.
- For the mast and boat stripe (A6 and D1), put the top **two** fabrics on the bottom of the pile.
- For the boat and pennant (A4, D2, and D3), put the top **three** fabrics on the bottom of the pile.
- All of the background pieces (A2, A3, A5, B2, B3, C, D4, and D5) stay where they started.

5. To sew the block back together, join the pieces into four sections (A–D) as described below. Refer to the pattern to make sure you sew the correct edges together and follow the dots for placement between sections.

- **Section A.** Stitch A1 to A2, keeping the seam adjacent to A6 straight. Add A3, centering it on top of A1/A2. Before adding A4, straighten the seam along the mast. Add A4, and then A5, keeping the seam adjacent to A6 straight. Center A6 on top of A1–A5 and stitch.
- **Section B.** Stitch B1 to B2, keeping the seam adjacent to section A straight. Add B3, keeping the seam adjacent to section A straight.
- **Section D.** Center D2 on top of D1 and stitch. Center D3 on top of D1 and stitch. Add D4, trying to keep the seam adjacent to section B straight. Add D5, trying to keep the seam adjacent to section A straight.

6. Straighten the edges before stitching one section to another section, making sure to only trim the edges you're sewing. Join the sections as follows.

- **Join A and B,** aligning A1 with B1.
- **Add C to A/B,** centering it on top of A/B.
- **Add D to A/B/C,** centering the mast (piece A6) on top of the boat.

7. Press and square up the block to measure 9½" x 9½", centering the boat.

8. Embroider or use a permanent pen to write "Love 2 Quilt" on the pennant of the flag. Embroider or use a permanent pen to write "USS One Sister," or the name of your favorite boat(s) along the boat stripe.

9. Repeat to make a total of seven blocks.

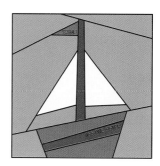

Make 7.

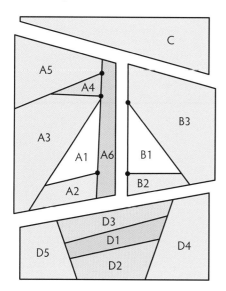

MAKING THE HOUSEBOAT BLOCKS

Refer to "General Craziness" for detailed instructions.

1. Stack the six fat quarters for the houseboat in a pile, right side up. As you stack, align the selvage and left side of each fat quarter. Every four fabrics will be together in the same block. Starting on the bottom, you can think: boat and windows, house and chimney, followed by roof and smokestack, and then the fourth fabric in each block is the background.

2. Trace the houseboat pattern on pattern sheets 1 and 2 onto the uncoated side of the freezer paper. Be sure to trace all the lines and to label each section. Press a freezer-paper pattern onto the top of the stack of fat quarters.

3. Using a rotary cutter and ruler, cut the block from the stack, cutting through the freezer paper and the entire stack of fabric. Note that the sections are labeled alphabetically. Start by cutting section F from the rest of the block. Then cut sections A/B from C/D/E. Finish cutting the pattern apart into sections A through F. (I say the alphabet backward and count backward to determine the cutting order.) Continue cutting until all the individual pieces have been separated. As you cut out each piece, stack the pieces on the master to stay organized.

4. Remove the freezer paper from all the pieces. Next you'll shuffle the pattern pieces as detailed below so that each element will be a different fabric.

   - For the roof and smokestack (D1 and E1), put the top fabric on the bottom of the pile.
   - For the house, chimney, and boat stripe (A1, A3, A4, B1, B3, B4, B5, C1, and F2), put the top *two* fabrics on the bottom of the pile.
   - For the boat and windows (A2, B2, F1, and F3), put the top *three* fabrics on the bottom of the pile.
   - The background pieces (A5, B6, C2, C3, D2, D3, E2, E3, F4, and F5) stay where they started.

5. To sew the block together, join the pieces into six sections (A–F) as described below. Refer to the pattern to make sure you sew the correct edges together and follow the dots for placement between sections.

   - **Section A.** Join A1 to A2, trying to keep the seam adjacent to A4 straight. Add A3, trying to keep the seam adjacent to A4 straight. Center A4 on top of A1/A2/A3 and stitch. Center A5 on top of A4 and stitch.
   - **Sections B.** Join B1 to B2, trying to keep the seam adjacent to B4 straight. Add B3, keeping the seam adjacent to B4 straight. Add B4, keeping the seam adjacent to section F straight. Before adding B5, straighten the edge of B1/B2/B3. Center B5 on top of B1/B2/B3 and stitch. Center B6 on top of B5 and stitch.
   - **Section C.** Join C1 to C2, trying to keep the seam adjacent to section D straight. Add C3, keeping the seam adjacent to section D straight.
   - **Section D.** Join D1 to D2, trying to keep the seam adjacent to D3 straight. Add D3, trying to keep the seam adjacent to section C straight.
   - **Section E.** Stitch E1 to E2, trying to keep the seam adjacent to E3 straight. Add E3, trying to keep the seam adjacent to section B straight.
   - **Section F.** Center F2 on top of F1 and stitch. Center F3 on top of F1/F2 and stitch. Add F3, centering the edges. Before adding F4 and F5, straighten both edges of F1/F2/F3. Center F4 on top of F1/F2/F3 and stitch. Center F5 on top of F1/F2/F3 and stitch.

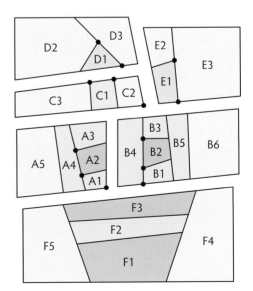

6. Straighten the edges before stitching one section to another section, making sure to only trim the edges you're sewing. Join the sections as follows.

- **Join A and B,** keeping the seam adjacent to section F straight.
- **Join C and D,** centering D1 on top of C1.
- **Add E to C/D,** trying to keep the seam adjacent to section B straight.
- **Stitch C/D/E to A/B,** centering C1 and E1 on top of the house portion of A/B.
- **Stitch A/B/C/D/E to F,** centering the house portion of section A/B over F3.

7. Press and square up the block to measure 9½" x 9½", centering the boat.

8. Referring to "Fusible Wool Appliqué" on page 11 and using the moon pattern on pattern sheet 1, fuse a gold moon in place on the chimney (C1). Using matching thread, whipstitch the moon in place.

9. Embroider or use a permanent pen to write "USS SoKozy," or the name of your favorite boat(s), along the boat stripe.

10. Repeat to make a total of six blocks.

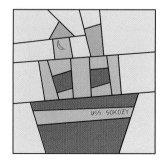

Make 6.

MAKING THE MOTORBOAT BLOCKS

Refer to "General Craziness" for detailed instructions.

1. Stack the six fat quarters for the motorboats in a pile, right side up. As you stack, align the selvage and left side of each fat quarter. Every four fabrics will be together in the same block. Starting on the bottom, you can think: boat, smokestack, and flagpole; house; windows, flag, and trim; then the fourth fabric in each block is the background.

2. Trace the motorboat pattern on pattern sheet 2 onto the uncoated side of the freezer paper. Be sure to trace all the lines and to label each section. Press a freezer-paper pattern onto the top of the stack of fat quarters.

3. Using a rotary cutter and ruler, cut the block from the stack, cutting through the freezer paper and the entire stack of fabric. Note that the sections are labeled alphabetically. Start cutting at the letter closest to the end of the alphabet and work backward until you get to A. (I say the alphabet backward and count backward to determine the cutting order.) Continue cutting until all the individual pieces have been separated. As you cut out each piece, stack the pieces on the master to stay organized.

4. Remove the freezer paper from all the pieces. Next you'll shuffle the pattern pieces so that each element will be a different fabric.

- For the windows, flag, and trim (A2, B2, C2, D1, and F1), put the top fabric on the bottom of the pile.
- For the house (A1, A3, A4, B1, B3, B4, and B5), put the top **two** fabrics on the bottom of the pile.
- For the boat, smokestack, and flagpole (C1, C3, D3, and G1), put the top **three** fabrics on the bottom of the pile.
- All of the background pieces (C4, C5, C6, D2, D4, D5, D6, E, F2, F3, G2, and G3) stay where they started.

5. To sew the block back together, join the pieces into seven sections (A–G) as described below. Refer to the pattern to make sure you sew the correct edges together and follow the dots for placement between sections.

- **Section A.** Stitch A1 to A2, keeping the seam adjacent to A4 straight. Add A3, keeping the seam adjacent to A4 straight. Add A4, keeping the seam adjacent to section F straight.

- **Section B.** Stitch B1 to B2, keeping the seam adjacent to B4 straight. Add B3, keeping the seam adjacent to B4 straight. Add B4, keeping the seam adjacent to section F straight. Before adding B5, straighten the edges of B1/B2/B3. Center B5 on top of B1/B2/B3 and stitch.

- **Section C.** Stitch C1 to C2, keeping the seam adjacent to C4 straight. Add C3, keeping the seam adjacent to C4 straight. Add C4, centering the edges as you sew. Before adding C5, straighten the edges of C1/C2/C3. Center C5 on top of C1/C2/C3 and stitch. Before adding C6, straighten the edges of C3/C4/C5. Center C6 on top of C1–C5 and stitch.

- **Section D.** Stitch D1 to D2, keeping the seam adjacent to D3 straight. Center D3 on top of D1/D2 and stitch. Before adding D4, straighten the edges of D1/D2. Center D4 on top of D1/D2 and stitch. Before adding D5, straighten the edges of D1/D3/D4. Center D5 on top of D1/D3/D4 and stitch. Before adding D6, straighten the edges of D3/D5. Center D6 on top of D3/D5 and stitch.

- **Section F.** Stitch F1 to F2, keeping the seam adjacent to section B straight. Add F3, keeping the seam adjacent to section D straight.

- **Section G.** Stitch G1 to G2, keeping the seam adjacent to section F straight. Add G3, keeping the seam adjacent to section F straight.

6. Straighten the edges before stitching one section to another sections, making sure to only trim the edges you're sewing. Join the sections as follows.

- **Join A to B,** keeping the seam adjacent to section F straight.

- **Add C to A/B,** keeping the seam adjacent to section D straight.

- **Add D to A/B/C,** keeping the seam adjacent to section F straight.

- **Add E to A/B/C/D,** centering it on top of A/B/C/D.

- **Join F to G,** centering F1 on top of G1.

- **Join A/B/C/D/E to F/G,** positioning the house portion toward the front of the boat.

7. Press and square up the block to measure 7½" x 9½", centering the boat.

8. Sew a 2½" x 9½" rectangle of matching background fabric to the top of the motorboat block so that the block measures 9½" x 9½".

9. Repeat to make a total of six Motorboat blocks.

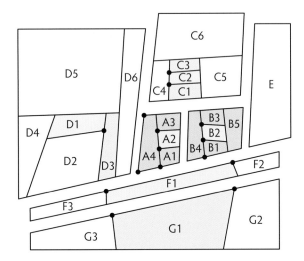

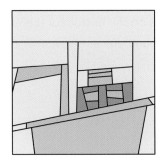

Make 6.

MAKING THE PARTY BARGE BLOCKS

Refer to "General Craziness" for detailed instructions.

1. Stack the six fat quarters for the party barges in a pile, right side up. As you stack, align the selvage and left side of each fat quarter. Every four fabrics will be together in the same block. Starting on the bottom, you can think: pontoon, windows, and roof; boat; house; and then the fourth fabric in each block is the background.

2. Trace the party-barge pattern on pattern sheet 4 onto the uncoated side of the freezer paper. Be sure to trace all the lines and to label each section. Press a freezer-paper pattern onto the top of the stack of fat quarters.

3. Using a rotary cutter and ruler, cut the block from the stack, cutting through the freezer paper and the entire stack of fabric. Note that the sections are labeled alphabetically. Start cutting at the letter closest to the end of the alphabet, and work backward, until you get to A. (I say the alphabet backward and count backward to determine the cutting order.) Continue cutting until all the individual pieces have been separated. As you cut out each piece, stack the pieces on the master to stay organized.

4. Remove the freezer paper from all the pieces. Next you'll shuffle the pattern pieces so that each element will be a different fabric.

   - For the pontoon, windows, and cabin top (A1, C2, C3, and D1), put the top fabric on the bottom of the pile.

   - For the boat (B1), put the top *two* fabrics on the bottom of the pile.

   - For the house (C1, C4, C5, C6, and C7), put the top *three* fabrics on the bottom of the pile.

   - The background pieces (A2, A3, A4, B2, B3, C8, C9, D2, D3, and D4) stay where they started.

5. To sew the block back together, join the pieces into four sections (A–D) as described below. Refer to the pattern to make sure you sew the correct edges together and follow the dots for placement between sections.

   - **Section A.** Stitch A1 to A2, keeping the seam adjacent to A3 straight. Add A3 and A4, keeping the seam adjacent to section B straight.

   - **Sections B.** Stitch B1 to B2, keeping the seam adjacent to section C straight. Add B3, keeping the seam adjacent to section C straight.

   - **Section C.** Stitch C1 to C2, keeping the seam adjacent to C6 straight. Add C3, C4, and C5 in numerical order, keeping the seam adjacent to C6 straight. Center C6 on top of C1–C5 and stitch. Before adding C7, straighten the edges of C1–C5. Center C7 on top of C1–C5 and stitch. Before adding C8, straighten the edges of C5/C6/C7. Center C8 on top of C5/C6/C7 and stitch. Before adding C9, straighten the edges of C4/C6/C7. Center C9 on top of C4/C6/C7 and stitch.

   - **Section D.** Center D1 on top of D2 and stitch. Before adding D3 and D4, straighten both edges of D1/D2. Add D3 and D4, keeping the seam adjacent to section C straight.

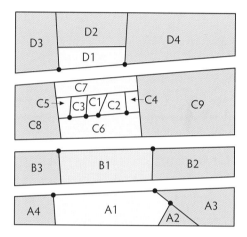

6. Straighten the edges before stitching one section to another sections, making sure to only trim the edges you're sewing. Join the sections as follows.

   - **Join A to B,** centering the boat (piece B1) on top of the house (piece A1).

   - **Join C and D,** centering the roof (piece D1) on top of the house (piece C7).

    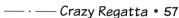

- **Straighten the bottom edge of section C.** Referring to "Fusible Wool Appliqué" and using the patterns on pattern sheet 4, fuse a brown palm-tree trunk and green palm-tree leaves in place on C9, making sure to check the location in relation to the boat (B1) so the tree is in the boat.
- **Stitch A/B to C/D,** centering the house and palm tree on top of the boat (B1).

7. Using matching thread, whipstitch the palm tree in place.

8. Press and square up the block to measure 6½" x 9½".

9. Sew a 3½" x 9½" rectangle of matching background fabric to the top of the block so the block will measure 9½" x 9½".

10. Cut a 6" length of pom-poms. Sew the pom-poms to the roof of the party barge (D1) and tuck under each end.

11. Repeat to make a total of six Party Barge blocks.

Make 6.

MAKING THE WAVE BLOCKS

Refer to "General Craziness" for detailed instructions.

1. Stack 10 dark-blue and dark-green fat quarters in a pile, right side up. Repeat to make a second stack of 10 light-aqua fat quarters. Try to have contrast from one piece to the next, either by print or color. As you stack, align the selvage and left side of each fat quarter.

2. You'll cut four wave patterns from each fat quarter. Trace the wave pattern on page 60 four times onto the uncoated side of a piece of freezer paper, placing the patterns side by side with no space between the patterns. Repeat to make a second four-block pattern (you'll need one for each stack of fabric). Then trace the wave pattern one time to make an extra pattern to stack on. Be sure to trace all the lines and to label each section. Press a four-block freezer-paper pattern onto the top of each stack of fat quarters.

3. Using a rotary cutter and ruler, cut the block from each stack, cutting through the freezer paper and the entire stack of fabric. Note that the sections are labeled alphabetically. Start cutting at the letter closest to the end of the alphabet and work backward until you get to A. (I say the alphabet backward and count backward to determine the cutting order.) Continue cutting until all the individual pieces have been separated. As you cut out each piece, stack the pieces on its own master to stay organized.

4. You should have two stacks of Wave blocks: one with all light fabrics and one with all dark fabrics. Trade the dark A2, B1, C3, C4, D1, D2, E1, and E2 pieces with the light A2, B1, C3, C4, D1, D2, and E2 pieces so that the wave pattern is visible in both stacks.

 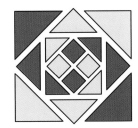

Light stack   Dark stack

 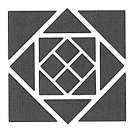

Trade dark and light pieces as instructed.

5. Remove the freezer paper from all the pieces. Next you'll shuffle the pattern pieces so that each element will be a different fabric.
- **A1 and B1,** put the top fabric on the bottom of the pile
- **A2 and B2,** put the top *two* fabrics on the bottom of the pile.
- **C1 and C3,** put the top *three* fabrics on the bottom of the pile.
- **C2 and C4,** put the top *four* fabrics on the bottom of the pile.
- **D1 and D3,** put the top *five* fabrics on the bottom of the pile.

- **D2 and D4,** put the top *six* fabrics on the bottom of the pile.
- **E1 and E3,** put the top *seven* fabrics on the bottom of the pile.
- **E2 and E4,** put the top *eight* fabrics on the bottom of the pile.

6. To sew the block back together, join the pieces into five sections (A–E) as described below. Refer to the pattern to make sure you sew the correct edges together. Prior to piecing, place a pin in each B2 so you can keep track of which end is up.

- **Sections A and B.** Stitch A1 to A2. Stitch B1 to B2. Press the seam allowances toward A1 and B2. Stitch A to B, matching the center seam. Square up the unit to 1½" x 1½".
- **Section C.** Center each piece by placing the point of a triangle on the center seam. Add each piece in numerical order. Square up unit A/B/C to 2" x 2" (or to one consistent size, leaving ¼" at each square-in-a-square point for the seam allowance).
- **Section D.** Stitch each piece in numerical order, centering the triangles. Square up unit A/B/C/D to 2½" x 2½" (or to one consistent size, leaving ¼" at each square-in-a-square point for a seam allowance).
- **Section E.** Center each piece by placing the point of a triangle on the center seam. Stitch each piece in numerical order.

7. Press and square up the block to measure 3½" x 3½".

8. Repeat to make a total of 80 blocks. Only 75 blocks are needed for this project. Save the remaining blocks for another project or use them to piece a cute backing for your quilt.

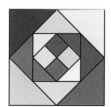

Make 80.

ASSEMBLING THE QUILT TOP

1. Lay out five boat blocks as shown in the quilt assembly diagram below. Sew the blocks together to make a block row. Press the seam allowances toward the left. Make a total of five rows.

2. To make the sashing rows, sew 15 Wave blocks together, rotating the blocks as shown in the quilt assembly diagram. Press the seam allowances to the right. Make a total of five rows.

3. Join the block rows and sashing rows as shown in the quilt assembly diagram. Press the seam allowances toward the block rows.

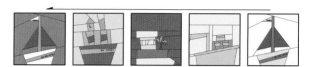

Quilt assembly

FINISHING THE QUILT

If you need help with any of the following finishing tasks, go to ShopMartingale.com/HowtoQuilt for free, downloadable information. Layer the quilt top with batting and backing; baste. Hand or machine quilt as desired. Use the assorted 2½"-wide strips to make and attach the binding.

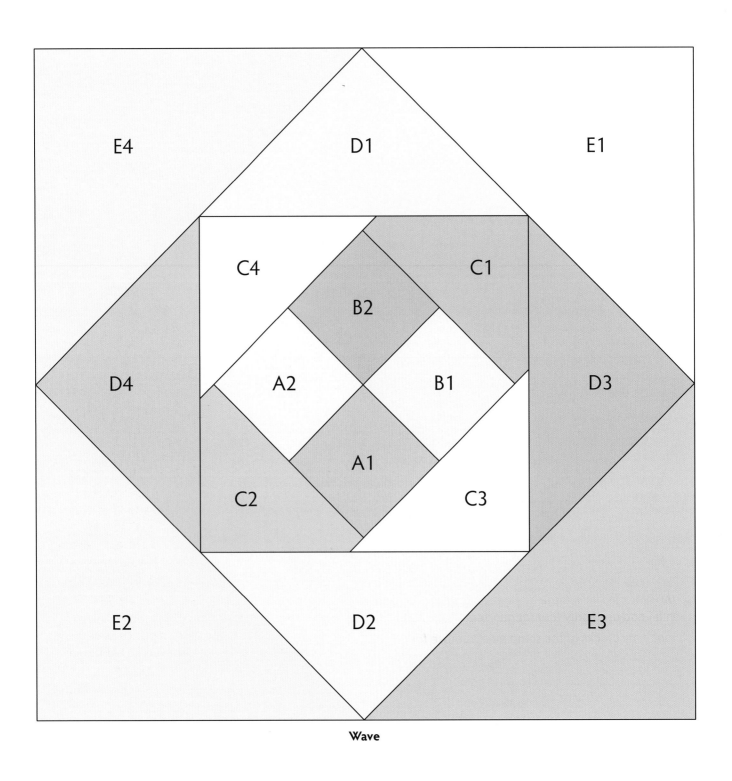

Wave

Welcome to the Lake

It's said that life's better at the lake, so welcome! Stop on in and join the fun.

MATERIALS

Yardage is based on 42"-wide fabric. Fat quarters measure 18" x 21".

1½ yards of blue plaid for letter background and quilt backing

¾ yard **each** of 4 assorted prints for Sun block*

4 fat quarters of assorted prints for Sailboat blocks**

10 squares, 8" x 8", of assorted dark-blue and dark-green prints for Wave blocks

10 squares, 8" x 8", of assorted light-aqua prints for Wave blocks

2 squares, 11" x 11", **each** of blue and gold prints for Star blocks (4 total)

3 strips, 2" x 42", **each** of red and cream prints for flag stripes (6 total)

⅜ yard of blue print for binding

12" x 24" rectangle of brown wool for letter appliqués

30" x 54" piece of batting

⅜ yard of 16"-wide paper-backed fusible web

Freezer paper

I used a leftover block from "Crazy Hot" on page 28, so the block in the sample on page 63 is scrappier than if I had used only four fat quarters.

**I made my blocks at the same time as those for "Crazy Regatta" on page 50, so blocks in the sample are scrappier than if I had used only four fat quarters.*

CUTTING

From *each* of the assorted prints for Sun blocks, cut:
   1 square, 27" x 27" (4 total)

From *each* of the red and cream strips, cut:
   1 strip, 1½" x 24½" (6 total)

From the *lengthwise grain* of the blue plaid, cut:
   1 strip, 6½" x 48½" (set aside the remaining piece for the quilt backing)

From the blue print for binding, cut:
   4 strips, 2½" x 42"

MAKING THE SAILBOAT BLOCKS

Before you begin, see "General Craziness" on page 5 for detailed instructions.

1. Stack the four fat quarters for the Sailboat blocks in a pile, right side up. As you stack, align the selvage and left side of each fat quarter. Every four fabrics will be together in the same block. Starting on the bottom, you can think: boat and pennant, mast and boat stripe, sail, and then the fourth fabric per block is the background.

2. Trace the sailboat pattern on pattern sheet 4 onto the uncoated side of the freezer paper. Be sure to trace all the lines and to label each section. Press the freezer-paper pattern onto the top of the stack of fat quarters.

3. Using a rotary cutter and ruler, cut the block out of the stack, cutting through the freezer paper and the entire stack of fabric. Note that the sections are labeled alphabetically. Start cutting at the letter closest to the end of the alphabet and work backward until you get to A. Continue cutting until all the individual pieces have been separated. As you cut out each piece, stack the pieces onto the master to help stay organized.

4. Remove the freezer paper from all the pieces. Next you'll shuffle the pattern pieces as detailed below, so that each element will be a different fabric.

   • For the sail (A1 and B1), put the top fabric on the bottom of the pile.

   • For the mast and boat stripe (A6 and D1), put the top **two** fabrics on the bottom of the pile.

   • For the boat and pennant (A4, D2, and D3), put the top **three** fabrics on the bottom of the pile.

   • The background pieces (A2, A3, A5, B2, B3, C, D4, and D5) stay where they started.

Pieced by Janet Nesbitt and Sandi McKell, quilted by Kathy Woods.
Finished size: 24½" x 48½" • Sun block size: 12" x 12" • Sailboat block size: 9" x 9"
Star block size: 6" x 6" • Wave block size: 3" x 3"

5. To sew the block back together, join the pieces into four sections (A–D) as described below. Refer to the pattern to make sure you sew the correct edges together and follow the dots for placement between sections.

- **Section A.** Stitch A1 to A2, keeping the seam adjacent to A6 straight. Add A3, centering it on top of A1/A2. Before adding A4, straighten the seam along the mast. Add A4, and then A5, keeping the seam adjacent to A6 straight. Center A6 on top of A1–A5 and stitch.

- **Sections B.** Stitch B1 to B2, keeping the seam adjacent to section A straight. Add B3, keeping the seam adjacent to section A straight.

- **Section D.** Center D2 on top of D1 and stitch. Center D3 on top of D1 and stitch. Add D4, trying to keep the seam adjacent to section B straight. Add D5, trying to keep the seam adjacent to section A straight.

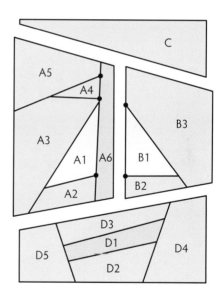

6. Straighten the edges before stitching one section to another section, making sure to only trim the edges you're sewing. Join the sections as follows.

- **Join A and B,** aligning A1 with B1.
- **Add C to A/B,** centering it on top of A/B.
- **Add D to A/B/C,** centering the mast (piece A6) on top of the boat.

7. Press and square up the block to measure 9½" x 9½", centering the boat.

8. Embroider or use a permanent pen to write "Love 2 Quilt" on the flag pennant. Embroider or use a permanent pen to write "USS One Sister," or the name of your favorite boat(s), on the boat stripe.

9. Repeat to make a total of four blocks.

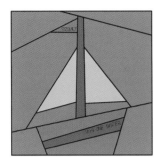

Make 4.

MAKING THE WAVE BLOCKS

Refer to "General Craziness" on page 5 for detailed instructions.

1. Stack the dark-blue and dark-green 8" squares in a pile, right side up. Repeat to make a second stack of the light-aqua 8" squares. Try to have contrast from one piece to the next, either by print or color. As you stack, align the bottom and left side of each square.

2. Trace the wave pattern on page 60 three times (one for each stack of fabric, plus one extra to stack on) onto the uncoated side of a piece of freezer paper. Be sure to trace all the lines and to label each section. Press a freezer-paper pattern onto the top of each stack of squares.

3. Using a rotary cutter and ruler, cut the block from each stack, cutting through the freezer paper and the entire stack of fabric. Note that the sections are labeled alphabetically. Start cutting at the letter closest to the end of the alphabet and work backward until you get to A. Continue cutting until all the individual pieces have been separated. As you cut out each piece, stack the pieces on the master to help stay organized.

4. You should have two stacks of Wave blocks: one with all light fabrics and one with all dark. Swap the dark A2, B1, C3, C4, D1, D2, E1, and E2 pieces with the light A2, B1, C3, C4, D1, D2, E1, and E2 pieces so the wave pattern's visible in both stacks.

5. Remove the freezer paper from all the pieces. Next you'll shuffle the pattern pieces so that each element will be a different fabric.

- **A1 and B1,** put the top fabric on the bottom of the pile.
- **A2 and B2,** put the top *two* fabrics on the bottom of the pile.
- **C1 and C3,** put the top *three* fabrics on the bottom of the pile.
- **C2 and C4,** put the top *four* fabrics on the bottom of the pile.
- **D1 and D3,** put the top *five* fabrics on the bottom of the pile.
- **D2 and D4,** put the top *six* fabrics on the bottom of the pile.
- **E1 and E3,** put the top *seven* fabrics on the bottom of the pile.
- **E2 and E4,** put the top *eight* fabrics on the bottom of the pile.

6. To sew the block back together, join the pieces into five sections (A–E) as described below. Remember to refer to the pattern to make sure you sew the correct edges together. Prior to piecing, place a pin in each B2 so you can keep track of which end is up.

- **Sections A and B.** Stitch A1 to A2. Stitch B1 to B2. Press the seam allowances toward A1 and B2. Join A and B, matching the center seam. Square up the unit to 1½" x 1½".

- **Section C.** Center each piece by placing the point of a triangle on the center seam. Add each piece in numerical order. Square up unit A/B/C to 2" x 2" (or to one consistent size, leaving ¼" at each square-in-a-square point for the seam allowance).

- **Section D.** Stitch each piece in numerical order, centering the triangles. Square up unit A/B/C/D to 2½" x 2½" (or to one consistent size, leaving ¼" at each square-in-a-square point for the seam allowance).

- **Section E.** Center each piece by placing the point of a triangle on the center seam. Stitch each piece in numerical order.

7. Press and square up the block to measure 3½" x 3½".

8. Repeat to make a total of 20 blocks.

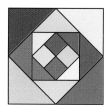

Make 20.

MAKING THE CRAZY STAR BLOCKS

Before you begin, see "General Craziness" on page 5 for detailed instructions.

1. Stack the four squares for the stars in a pile, right side up. As you stack, align the bottom and left side of each square. Try to have contrast from one piece to the next, either by print or color. Every two fabrics will be together in the same block

2. Trace the star pattern on pages 18 and 19 onto the uncoated side of a piece of freezer paper. Be sure trace all lines and to label each section. Press a freezer-paper pattern onto the top of the stack of squares.

3. Using a rotary cutter and ruler, cut the block from the stack, cutting through the freezer paper and the entire stack of fabric. Start cutting at the letter closest to the end of the alphabet and work backward until you get to A. (I say the alphabet backward and count backward to determine the cutting order.) Continue cutting until all the individual pieces have been separated. As you cut out each piece, stack the pieces on the master.

4. Remove the freezer paper from all the pieces. Next you'll shuffle the pattern pieces among the stacks so that each element is a different fabric.

- Move the star points (A2, A3, B1, C1, and D1), putting the top fabric to the bottom of the stack.

- Move the star center (A1), putting the top *two* fabrics to the bottom of the stack.

- All of the background pieces (B2, C2, C3, D2, and D3) stay where they started.

5. To sew the block back together, join the pieces into four sections (A–D) as described below. (See "Matching Diagonal Seams" on page 10.) Refer to the pattern to make sure you sew the correct edges together and follow the dots for placement between sections.

- **Section A.** Center A2 on top of A1 and stitch. Center A3 on top of A1/A2 and stitch.

- **Section B.** Stitch B1 to B2, keeping the seam adjacent to section A straight (noted by dot on pattern).

- **Section C.** Stitch C1 to C2, and then add C3, trying to keep the inside seam adjacent to section A straight (noted by dot on pattern). Straighten the C1/C2 edge before adding C3.

- **Section D.** Stitch D1 to D2, and then add piece D3, trying to keep the inside seam adjacent to section A straight (noted by dot on pattern). Straighten the D1/D2 edge before adding D3.

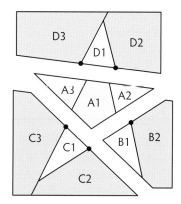

6. Straighten the edges before stitching one section to another section, making sure to only trim the edges you're sewing. Join the sections as follows.

- **Join A and B,** matching the star point seams.
- **Add C to A/B,** centering the edge of C1 with A1. The seam intersections probably won't match up.
- **Add D to A/B/C,** centering D1 with A1. Again, the seam intersections won't necessarily match.

7. Press and square up the block to measure 6½" x 6½", centering the star.

8. Make four blocks, two with blue backgrounds and two with gold backgrounds. Only two blocks are needed for this project. Save the remaining blocks for another project or use them to piece a cute backing for your quilt.

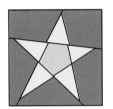 

Make 2 of each.

MAKING THE CRAZY SUN BLOCKS

Before you begin, see "General Craziness" on page 5 for detailed instructions.

1. Stack the four fabrics for the Sun blocks in a pile, right side up. Every four fabrics will be together in the same block. As you stack, align the selvage and left side of each fabric.

2. A complete Sun block is made up of four Crazy-sun quadrants. Trace the sun-quadrant pattern on pattern sheet 3 four times onto the uncoated side of a piece of freezer paper, placing the patterns side by side with no space between the patterns and rotating the patterns to make a full Sun block. (You can press two pieces of freezer paper together so the freezer paper is big enough to trace the full sun pattern.) Press a full sun pattern onto the top of the stack of fabric.

3. Using a rotary cutter and ruler, cut the block from the stack, cutting through the freezer paper and the entire stack of fabric. Cut the Sun block apart into the four quadrants. Cut and piece each quadrant before proceeding to the next quadrant. Start by cutting off section H. Next cut the top half of the block (A/B/C) from the bottom half (D/E/F/G). Then cut the pattern apart into sections A through G. (I say the alphabet backward and count backward to determine

the cutting order.) Continue cutting until all the individual pieces have been separated. As you cut out each piece, stack the pieces the master.

4. Remove the freezer paper from all the pieces. Shuffle the pieces among the stacks as detailed below so there are four different fabrics in the block.
- For the rays (A1, B1, C3, D1, E1, F1, and G1), put the top fabric on the bottom of the stack.
- For the circle (B2, C2, E2, and F2), put the top **two** fabrics on the bottom of the stack.
- For the center star (C1 and H), put the top **three** fabrics on the bottom of the stack.
- All of the background pieces (A2, A3, A4, D2, D3, D4, G2, G3, and G4) stay where they started.

5. To sew the block back together, join the pieces into seven sections (A–G) as described below. Refer to the pattern to make sure you sew the correct edges together and follow the dots for placement between sections.
- **Section A.** Stitch A1 to A2, trying to keep the seam adjacent to A4 straight. Straighten the edge before adding A3. Add A3, trying to keep the seam adjacent to A4 straight. Center A4 on top of A1/A2/A3 and stitch.
- **Section B.** Stitch B1 to B2, trying to keep the edge adjacent to section A straight.
- **Section C.** Stitch C1 to C2, trying to keep the edge adjacent to C3 straight. Center C3 on top of C1/C2 and stitch.
- **Section D.** Stitch D1 to D2, trying to keep the edge adjacent to D4 straight. Straighten the edge

before adding D3. Add D3, trying to keep the edge adjacent to D4 straight. Center D4 on top of D1/D2/D3 and stitch.

- **Section E.** Stitch E1 to E2, trying to keep the edge adjacent to section D straight.
- **Section F.** Center F2 on top of F1 and stitch.
- **Section G.** Stitch G1 to G2, trying to keep the edge adjacent to G4 straight. Straighten the edge before adding G3. Add G3, trying to keep the edge adjacent to G4 straight. Add G4, centering it on top of G1/G2/G3.

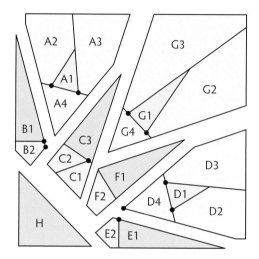

6. Straighten the edges before stitching one section to another section, making sure to only trim the edges you're sewing. Join the sections as follows.

- **Trim both A4 edges.** Join A and B, keeping the edge adjacent to C straight. Trim A/B, making sure you have ¼" seam allowance at B2.
- **Add C to A/B,** matching the seam intersection for the circle at B2 and C2.
- **Trim both D4 edges.** Join D to E, keeping the edge adjacent to F straight. Trim D/E, making sure you have a ¼" seam allowance at E2.
- **Add F to D/E,** matching the seam intersection for the circle at E2 and F2.
- **Trim both G4 edges.** Add G to D/E/F, keeping the edge adjacent to C straight.
- **Trim A/B/C,** making sure you have a ¼" seam allowance at C2. Join A/B/C to D/E/F/G, matching the seam intersection for the circle at F2 and C2.
- **Add H,** centering the edge of H on the inner circle (B2, C1, C2, E2, and F2).

7. Repeat to make four matching quadrants for one block.

8. Trim the two inside edges of the quadrant as shown in step 9 on page 31, positioning a ruler so that the seams for the inner circle (B2 and E2) are 2¾" from the upper-right corner. The points of the rays (B1 and E1) should be about 7" from the corner on the ruler, which gives you a ¼" seam allowance along the edge of the block after trimming. Your blocks may be larger or smaller, but pick consistent numbers for each set of four quadrants. For the circle to appear round and the points to match, it's important to use a consistent measurement for each set of four quadrants.

9. Join the quadrants, matching the center seam intersections and the seams for the inner circle. Try to match the sun points (B1 and E1), but don't worry if they don't match exactly.

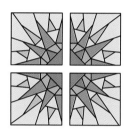 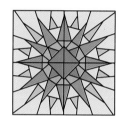

10. Press and square up the block to measure 12½" x 12½".

11. Repeat to make a total of four blocks. Only one block is required for this project. Save the remaining blocks for another project or use them to piece a cute backing for your quilt.

ASSEMBLING THE QUILT TOP

1. For the flag stripes, join the cream and red 1½"-wide strips along their long edges, alternating the red and cream strips. Press the seam allowances toward the red strips.

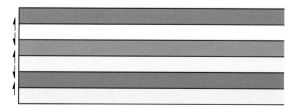

2. Stitch two Star blocks to the left of the flag stripes. Press the seam allowances toward the Star blocks.

3. Join the Sailboat blocks side by side. Press the seam allowances to the right. Then sew the step 2 section to the top of the Sailboat blocks. Press the seam allowances toward the top section.

4. Join four Wave blocks side by side. Press the seam allowances to the left. Stitch the wave strip to the bottom of the Sun block. Press the seam allowances toward the Wave blocks.

5. Sew the section from step 4 to the left of the section from step 3. Press the seam allowances toward the Sailboat/Star blocks.

6. Join 16 Wave blocks side by side to make a strip. Press the seam allowances in one direction. Sew the strip to the bottom of the quilt top. Press the seam allowances toward the Sailboat blocks.

7. Referring to "Fusible Wool Appliqué" on page 11 and using the letter patterns on pages 69 and 70, cut out the letters from the brown wool. Using matching thread, whipstitch the greeting to the blue-plaid strip. Sew the appliquéd strip to the bottom of the quilt top. Press the seam allowances toward the blue-plaid strip.

FINISHING THE QUILT

If you need help with any of the following finishing tasks, go to ShopMartingale.com/HowtoQuilt for free, downloadable information. Layer the quilt top with batting and backing; baste. Hand or machine quilt as desired. Use the blue 2½"-wide strips to make and attach the binding.

Quilt assembly

Cut 3.

Cut 1.

Cut 1.

Cut 1.

Appliqué patterns do not
include seam allowances.

Cut 1.

Cut 2.

Cut 2.

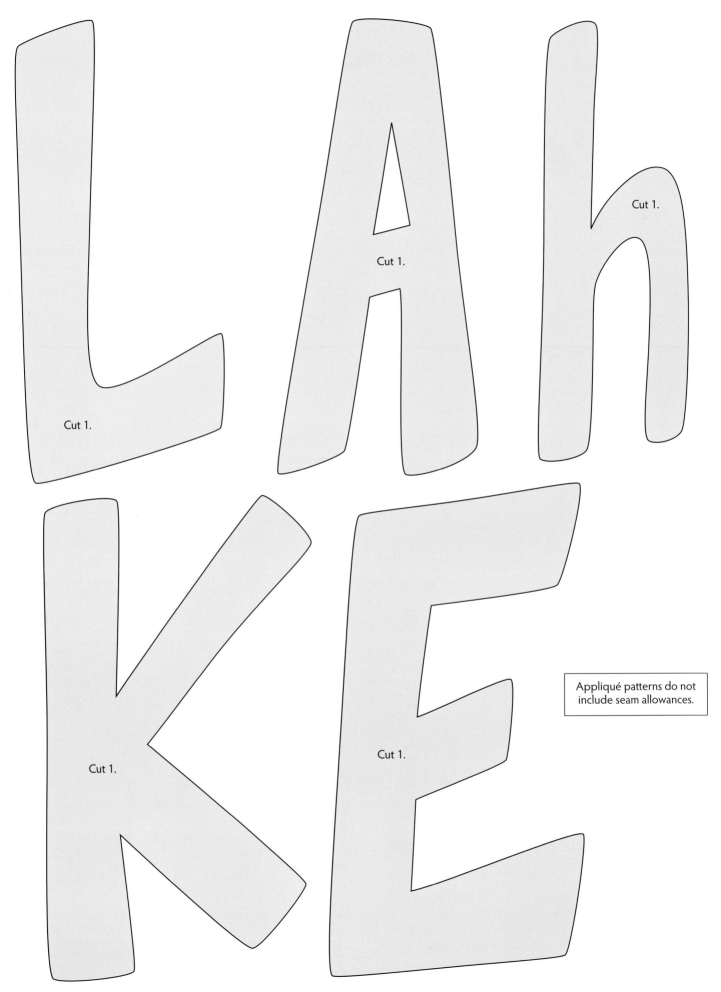

Cut 1.

Cut 1.

Cut 1.

Cut 1.

Cut 1.

Appliqué patterns do not include seam allowances.

Crazy Moose Messages

I had fun making these guys and dressing them up. My friend's maiden name is Moos (without the "e"), and she just had a milestone birthday, so it seemed appropriate that she be selected as the lucky recipient of the very first moose message! I hope you have the "moost" fun making these moose.

MATERIALS

Yardage is based on 42"-wide fabric.

⅔ yard **each** of 8 assorted brown prints and/or plaids for Moose blocks

⅔ yard **each** of 8 assorted light to medium prints and/or plaids for Moose blocks and scrappy binding*

1¼ yards of dark-brown plaid for border

7" x 8" rectangle **each** of 4 assorted blue wools for letter appliqués

Scraps of assorted wools for appliqué motifs

4 yards of fabric for backing

70" x 78" piece of batting

½ yard of 16"-wide paper-backed fusible web (optional)

Black and ecru embroidery floss for messages

32 buttons, ³⁄₁₆" diameter, for moose eyes

Freezer paper

*You'll need color pairs consisting of 2 red, 2 blue, 2 teal, and 2 green prints and/or plaids.

CUTTING

From the dark-brown plaid, cut:
　7 strips, 6½" x 42"

From the assorted light to medium prints and/or plaids, cut a *total* of:
　15 strips, 2½" x 20"

MAKING THE BLOCKS

Before you begin, see "General Craziness" on page 5 for detailed instructions.

1. Stack the eight brown fabrics in a pile, right side up. Make a second pile of eight light/medium fabrics in another pile, right side up. Stack the light/mediums together in color groups: reds, blues, teals, and greens. As you stack, align the selvage and left side of each fabric.

PLAN AHEAD

Normally with these blocks it's difficult to predict which fabrics will be together in the same blocks, but this time you can! So, if you'd like to control your fabric choices, the fabrics on the bottom of each pile will be together in a block. Then the next "layer" of fabrics (the fabrics second from the bottom) will be together in a block, etc. Look at each layer as you stack them up to make sure you like your combination of fabrics and that they contrast with each other. In addition, every two fabrics in each stack of lights and darks will be together in the same block, paired as body and antlers, and therefore need to contrast.

2. Trace the two halves of the moose pattern on pattern sheets 1 and 3 three times (one for each stack of fabric plus one extra to stack on) onto the uncoated side of a piece of freezer paper. Be sure to trace all lines and to label each section. Press the freezer-paper pattern halves together to make a whole block. Then press a freezer-paper pattern onto the top of each stack of fabric.

Pieced by Janet Nesbitt, wool appliquéd by Sandy McKell, and quilted by Kathy Woods.

Finished size: 72½" x 64½" • **Block size:** 15" x 13"

3. Using a rotary cutter and ruler, cut the block from each stack of fabric, cutting through the freezer paper and the entire stack of fabric. Note that the sections are labeled alphabetically. Start by cutting the right half of the block (sections A/B/C) from the left half of the block (sections D–S). Then separate the left half of the block into three sections: D/E/F, G/H/J/K/L/M, and N/O/P/Q/R/S. Continue cutting the block apart into 18 sections, A through S. (I say the alphabet backward and count backward to determine the cutting order.) Continue cutting until all the individual pieces have been separated. As you cut out each piece, stack the darks on one master and the lights on another master to stay organized. You should have two stacks of fabric.

4. Trade the pattern pieces among the stacks so you have a dark moose with light backgrounds in one stack and a light moose with dark backgrounds in the other stack. The moose pieces are: A1, B2, B4, B6, B7, C1, D1, D3, E1, F1, G1, H1, J1, K1, L1, M1, N1, O1, P1, and Q.

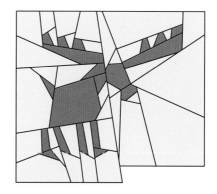

5. Remove the freezer paper from all the pieces. Next shuffle the fabric so that each element is a different fabric.

- **For the antlers in the dark stack only** (B2, B4, B6, B7, N1, O1, P1, and Q), put the top fabric on the bottom of the pile.

- **For the light stack:** Each moose will be one color, but have two different fabrics for the body and the antlers, so you have to shuffle differently than you normally do. For the antlers (B2, B4, B6, B7, N1, O1, P1, and Q), separate the pile into the four colors, laying the pieces out from left to right. Put the top fabric on the bottom for each of the four piles. Pick up the pieces in the same exact order, left to right, and place them on the master. You'll do this for each of the antler pieces.

Green top   Teal   Blue   Red bottom

- All other moose and background pieces stay where they started.

6. To sew the block back together, join the pieces into sections as described below. Remember to refer to the pattern to make sure you sew the correct edges together and follow the dots for placement between sections.

- **Section A.** Stitch A1 to A2, keeping the seam adjacent to section C straight. Center A3 on top of A1/A2 and stitch. Before adding A4, straighten the edges of A1/A3. Add A4, keeping the seam adjacent to section B straight.

- **Section B.** Stitch B1 to B2, keeping the seam adjacent to B7 straight. Add B3, B4, B5, and B6 in numerical order and keeping the seam adjacent to B7 straight. Add B7 and B8, keeping the inside seam adjacent to section A straight. Before adding B9, straighten the edges of B1–B6, and then add B9, keeping the seam adjacent to section A straight. Before adding B10, straighten the edges of B6/B7/B9. Add B10, keeping the seam adjacent to section C straight.

- **Section C.** Center C2 on top of C1 and stitch. Before adding C3, straighten the edges of C1/C2. Center C3 on top of C1/C2 and stitch. Before adding C4, straighten the edges of C1/C3. Add C4, keeping the seam adjacent to section A straight. Before adding C5, straighten the edges of C1/C2/C3. Add C5, keeping the seam adjacent to C6

straight. Add C6, keeping the seam adjacent to sections A and B straight.

- **Section D.** Stitch D1 to D2, keeping the seam adjacent to D3 straight. Add D3, keeping the seam adjacent to section E straight. Before adding D4, straighten the edges of D2/D3. Add D4, keeping the seam adjacent to sections A and C straight.

- **Sections E.** Stitch E1 to E2, keeping the seam adjacent to section D straight.

- **Section F.** Stitch F1 to F2, keeping the seam adjacent to section D straight. Before adding F3, straighten the edges of F1/F3. Add F3, keeping the seam adjacent to section D straight.

- **Section G.** Stitch G1 to G2, keeping the seam adjacent to section H straight.

- **Section H.** Stitch H1 to H2, keeping the seam adjacent to section J straight.

- **Section J.** Stitch J1 to J2, keeping the seam adjacent to J3 straight. Center J3 on top of J1/J2 and stitch.

- **Section K.** Stitch K1 to K2, keeping the seam adjacent to K3 straight. Center K3 on top of K1/K2 and stitch.

- **Section L.** Stitch L1 to L2, keeping the seam adjacent to section M straight (noted by dot on pattern). Add L3, keeping the seam adjacent to section M straight.

- **Section M.** Stitch M1 to M2, keeping the seam adjacent to M3 straight (noted by dot on pattern). Add M3, keeping the seam adjacent to section L straight.

- **Section N.** Stitch N1 to N2, keeping the seam adjacent to section Q straight. Center N3 on top of N1/N2 and stitch.

- **Section O.** Stitch O1 to O2, keeping the seam adjacent to section Q straight. Before adding O3, straighten the edges of O1/O2. Center O3 on top of O1/O2 and stitch.

- **Section P.** Stitch P1 to P2, keeping the seam adjacent to section Q straight. Before adding P3, straighten the edges of P1/P2. Center P3 on top of P1/P2 and stitch.

7. Straighten the edges before stitching one section to another section, making sure to only trim the edges you're sewing. Join the sections as follows.

- **Join A and B,** keeping the seam adjacent to section C straight. When straightening the edges of section A/B before adding section C, don't be alarmed if you don't have a ¼" seam allowance at the tip of the antler (B7); th e tip will be slightly flattened after adding section C.

- **Add C to A/B,** centering the muzzle/nose (C1) under the head (A1). The seam intersections won't necessarily match.

- **Join D to E,** keeping the seam adjacent to section A straight.

- **Add F to D/E,** matching the top of the tail seam (F1) with the top of the body seam (D3).

- **Join G to H,** keeping the seam adjacent to section J straight. Before adding J to G/H, straighten the top of section J at the top of the leg.

- **Add J to G/H,** keeping the seam adjacent to section D straight. Before adding K to G/H/J, straighten the top of section K at the top of the leg.

- **Add K to G/H/J,** keeping the seam adjacent to section D straight.

- **Join L to M,** centering the leg (L1) on the hoof (M1). The seam intersections won't necessarily match. Before adding L/M to G/H/J/K, straighten the top of section L at the top of the leg.

- **Join L/M to G/H/J/K,** keeping the seam adjacent to sections D and F straight.

- **Join G–M to D/E/F,** centering the legs under the body (D3).

- **Join N to O, and then add P,** keeping the seam adjacent to section Q straight.

- **Add Q,** keeping the inside seam adjacent to section A straight.

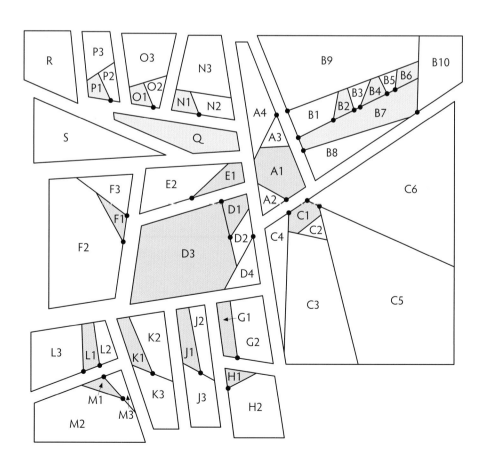

- **Add R to N/O/P/Q,** centering it on top of P1/P3/Q.

- **Add S to Q/R,** centering it on top of Q/R.

- **Before adding** the antler section (N–S) to the body/leg section (D–M), straighten the neck edge of the body. Then stitch the antler section to the body/legs section, keeping the seam adjacent to section A straight.

- **Stitch the right side** of the block (A/B/C) to the left side of the block (D–S), matching the top of the antler (Q) with the top of the head (A1).

8. Refer to "Fusible Wool Appliqué" on page 11 and using the patterns on pattern sheet 1 and pages 78 and 79, cut out the motifs from the assorted wool scraps. Using matching thread, whipstitch the motifs of your choice on the Moose blocks as shown in the photo on page 73.

9. Press and square up the block to measure 13½" x 15½" or to one consistent size. Repeat to make a total of 16 blocks.

ASSEMBLING THE QUILT TOP

1. Lay out the blocks in four rows of four blocks each as shown in the quilt assembly diagram below. Sew the blocks together in rows. Press the seam allowances in opposite directions from row to row. Join the rows. Press the seam allowances in one direction.

2. Join the dark-brown 6½"-wide strips end to end. From the pieced strip, cut two 52½"-long strips for the side borders and two 72½"-long strips for the top and bottom borders. Sew the side borders to the quilt top first, and then add the top and bottom borders. Press all seam allowances toward the border.

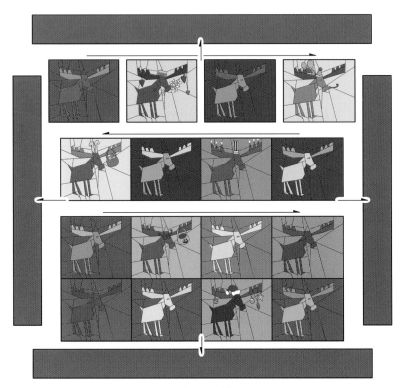

Quilt assembly

3. Refer to "Fusible Wool Appliqué." Using the letter patterns on pages 47–49 and the blue wool rectangles, make one each of letters M, a, k, h, m, s, L, and i. For the u, turn the n upside down. Make three of letters e and t. Make four of letter o and two of letter f. For the exclamation mark, make one lowercase l and add the period from the question mark. Make two apostrophes and two reversed apostrophes. Using matching thread, whipstitch the saying to the outer border as shown in the photo on page 73.

• MOOSE MESSAGES

You can use the same saying as I did, or you can choose a different message to appliqué on the border, such as *Have a "moost" Fabulous day!* or *Merry Christ "moose"!*

FINISHING THE QUILT

If you need help with any of the following finishing tasks, go to ShopMartingale.com/HowtoQuilt for free, downloadable information. Layer the quilt top with batting and backing; baste. Hand or machine quilt as desired. Use the assorted 2½"-wide strips to make and attach the binding.

• MAKE IT SMALLER

You can use 12 of the blocks in a smaller wall hanging and use the remaining four blocks to make four small quilts with individual messages. Or, make a nine-block wall hanging, leaving seven blocks to make with special messages and give as gifts!

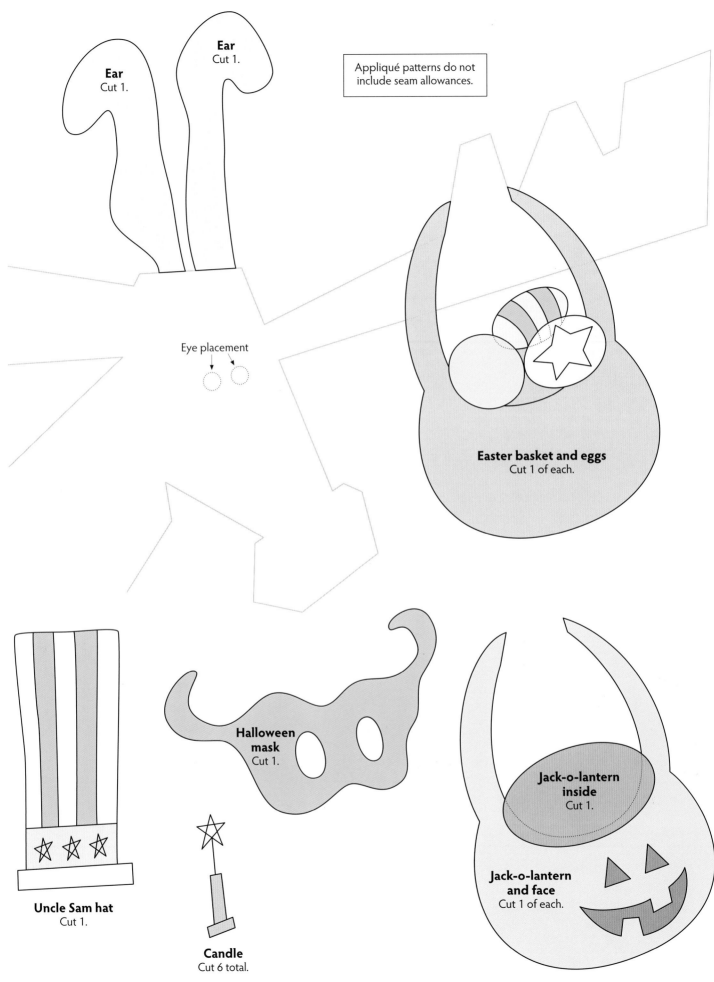

Ear
Cut 1.

Ear
Cut 1.

Appliqué patterns do not include seam allowances.

Eye placement

Easter basket and eggs
Cut 1 of each.

Halloween mask
Cut 1.

Jack-o-lantern inside
Cut 1.

Jack-o-lantern and face
Cut 1 of each.

Uncle Sam hat
Cut 1.

Candle
Cut 6 total.

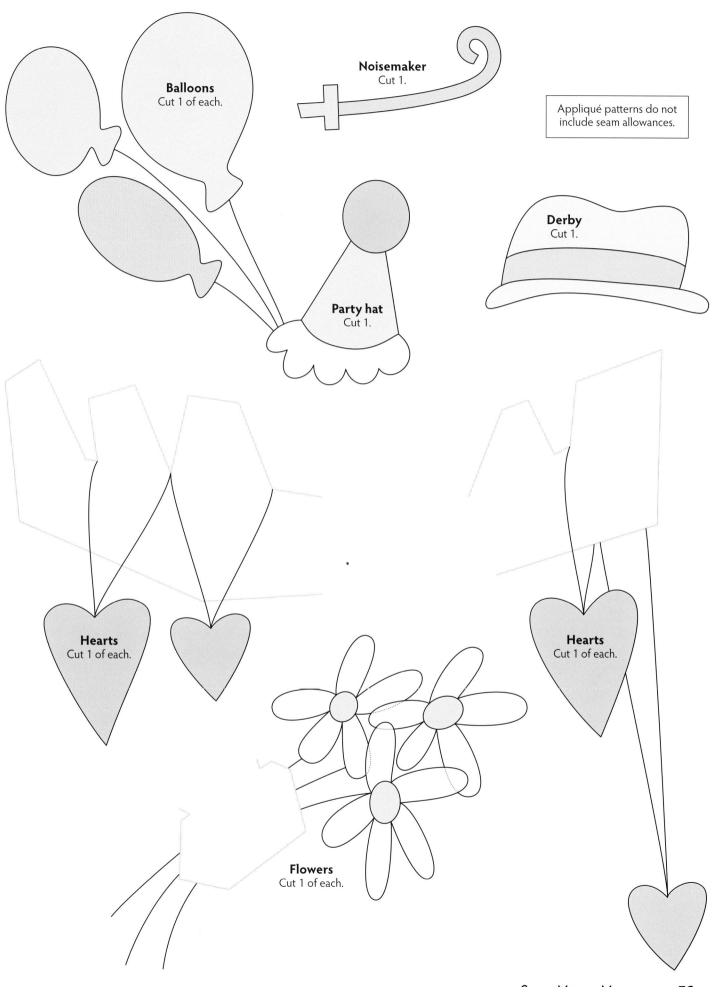

Balloons
Cut 1 of each.

Noisemaker
Cut 1.

Appliqué patterns do not include seam allowances.

Derby
Cut 1.

Party hat
Cut 1.

Hearts
Cut 1 of each.

Hearts
Cut 1 of each.

Flowers
Cut 1 of each.

Folk-Art Fireworks

Fireworks are a wonder to behold as they explode over the lake each Fourth of July. This quilt, too, is an explosion of my favorite textures and colors.

MATERIALS

Yardage is based on 42"-wide fabric.

⅞ yard **each** of 5 prints (1 dark red, 1 tomato-soup red, 1 blue, 1 gold, and 1 orange) for Crazy Sun blocks

3½ yards **total** of 32 assorted light prints for Star Wreath blocks and outer border

3¼ yards **total** of 84 assorted medium and dark prints for Star Wreath blocks and outer border

3⅜ yards of rust check for setting triangles, inner border, and binding

7⅞ yards of fabric for backing

90" x 90" piece of batting

Freezer paper

CUTTING

Instructions are for cutting 1 block at a time, which will make it easier to keep all the fabrics and pieces organized.

CUTTING FOR 1 STAR WREATH BLOCK

For each Star Wreath block, select 2 light prints for the background and 5 medium and/or dark prints. Number each fabric to correspond with the cutting and piecing diagrams.

From center light #1, cut:
  4 rectangles, 2" x 3½"
  4 squares, 2" x 2"

From outer light #2, cut:
  4 rectangles, 2" x 3½"
  12 squares, 2" x 2"
  4 squares, 2⅜" x 2⅜"; cut the squares in half diagonally to yield 8 half-square triangles

From center dark #1, cut:
  4 squares, 2" x 2"
  2 squares, 2⅜" x 2⅜"; cut the squares in half diagonally to yield 4 triangles

From center dark #2, cut:
  4 squares, 2" x 2"
  2 squares, 2⅜" x 2⅜"; cut the squares in half diagonally to yield 4 triangles

From outer dark #3, cut:
  4 squares, 2" x 2"
  2 squares, 2⅜" x 2⅜"; cut the squares in half diagonally to yield 4 triangles

From outer dark #4, cut:
  4 squares, 2" x 2"
  2 squares, 2⅜" x 2⅜"; cut the squares in half diagonally to yield 4 triangles

From outer dark #5, cut:
  8 squares, 3½" x 3½"

CUTTING FOR SETTING TRIANGLES, BORDERS, AND BINDING

From the rust check, cut:
  3 squares, 18¼" x 18¼"; cut the squares into quarters diagonally to yield 12 triangles
  2 squares, 9⅜" x 9⅜"; cut the squares in half diagonally to yield 4 triangles
  9 strips, 5½" x 42"
  9 strips, 2½" x 42"

From the assorted light prints, cut a *total* of:
  216 squares, 2" x 2"

From the assorted medium and dark prints, cut a *total* of:
  108 squares, 3½" x 3½"

Made by Gloria Brodhagen and quilted by Karen Brown.
Finished size: 84½" x 84½" • Block size: 12" x 12"

MAKING THE STAR WREATH BLOCKS

Instructions are for making one block.

1. With right sides together, sew dark #1 and #2 triangles together along their long edges to make four half-square-triangle units. Press the seam allowances toward the dark triangles. In the same way, sew light #2 and dark #3 triangles together to make four units. Sew light #2 and dark #4 triangles together to make four units.

Make 4 of each.

2. Sew dark #1/dark #2 units together as shown to make the center pinwheel unit. Make one. Press the seam allowances as indicated

3. Place a dark #1 square on the left end of a light #1 rectangle, right sides together. Sew diagonally from corner to corner as shown. Trim the excess corner fabric, leaving a ¼" seam allowance. Press the seam allowances toward the resulting triangle. Place a dark #2 square on the opposite

end. Sew diagonally from corner to corner as shown; press. Make four identical units.

Make 4.

4. Place a light #2 square on one corner of a dark #5 square. Sew diagonally from corner to corner as shown. Trim the excess corner fabric, leaving a ¼" seam allowance. Press the seam allowances toward the resulting triangle. In the same way, sew a light #2 square on an adjacent corner. Trim and press to complete the unit. Make four identical units.

Make 4.

5. Stitch a unit from step 3 to the bottom of a unit from step 4 as shown. Press the seam allowances in the direction indicated. Make four side units.

Make 4.

6. For the corner units, repeat step 4, placing a light #1 square on the upper-right corner of a dark #5 square. Sew, trim, and press. Place a dark #4 square on the upper-left corner of the dark #5 square as shown. Sew, trim, and press. Place a dark #3 square on the lower-right corner of the dark #5 square as shown. Sew, trim, and press. Make four identical units.

Make 4.

7. Lay out one corner unit, one dark #3 half-square-triangle unit, one dark #4 half-square-triangle unit, one light #2 square, and one light #2 rectangle as shown. Join the pieces into rows, and then join the rows, making sure to match the seam intersections. Press the seam allowance as indicated. Make four identical units.

Make 4.

8. Lay out four units from step 5, four units from step 7, and the center pinwheel unit as shown. Join the pieces into rows, making sure to match the seam intersections. Join the rows, making sure to match the seam intersections. Make a total of 20 blocks.

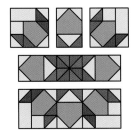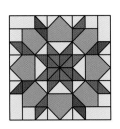

Make 20.

MAKING THE CRAZY SUN BLOCKS

Before you begin, see "General Craziness" on page 5 for detailed instructions.

1. Stack the five fabrics for the Crazy Sun blocks in a pile, right side up. Every four fabrics will be together in the same block. I started with gold on the bottom; then stacked dark red, orange, and blue, and ended with tomato-soup red on top. As you stack, align the selvage and left side of each fabric.

2. A complete Sun block is made up of four Crazy-sun quadrants. Trace the sun-quadrant pattern on pattern sheet 3 four times onto the uncoated side of a piece of freezer paper, placing the patterns side by side with no space between the patterns and rotating the patterns to make a full Sun. (You can press two pieces of freezer paper together so that the freezer paper is big enough to trace the full sun pattern.) Press a full sun pattern onto the top of the stack of fabrics.

3. Using a rotary cutter and ruler, cut the block from the stack, cutting through the freezer paper and the entire stack of fabric. Cut the Sun block apart into the four quadrants. Cut and piece each quadrant before proceeding to the next quadrant. Start by cutting off section H. Next cut the top half of the block (A/B/C) from the bottom half (D/E/F/G). Then cut the pattern apart into sections A through G. (I say the alphabet backward and count backward to determine the cutting order.) Continue cutting until all the individual pieces have been separated. As you cut out each piece, stack the pieces on the master to stay organized.

4. Remove the freezer paper from all the pieces. Shuffle the pattern pieces as detailed below so there are four different fabrics in each block.

- For the ray (A1, B1, C3, D1, E1, F1, and G1), put the top fabric on the bottom of the pile.

- For the circle pieces (B2, C2, E2, and F2), put the top *two* fabrics on the bottom of the pile.

- For the center star (C1 and H), put the top *three* fabrics on the bottom of each pile.

- All of the background pieces (A2, A3, A4, D2, D3, D4, G2, G3, and G4) stay where they started.

5. To sew the block back together, join the pieces into seven sections (A–G) as described below. Refer to the pattern to make sure you sew the correct edges together and follow the dots for placement between sections.

- **Section A.** Stitch A1 to A2, trying to keep the seam adjacent to A4 straight. Straighten the edge before adding A3. Add A3, trying to keep the seam adjacent to A4 straight. Center A4 on top of A1/A2/A3 and stitch.

- **Section B.** Stitch B1 to B2, trying to keep the edge adjacent to section A straight.

- **Section C.** Stitch C1 to C2, trying to keep the edge adjacent to C3 straight. Center C3 on top of C1/C2 and stitch.

- **Section D.** Stitch D1 to D2, trying to keep the edge adjacent to D4 straight. Straighten the edge before adding D3. Add D3, trying to keep the edge adjacent to D4 straight. Center D4 on top of D1/D2/D3 and stitch.

- **Section E.** Stitch E1 to E2, trying to keep the edge adjacent to section D straight.
- **Section F.** Center F2 on top of F1 and stitch.
- **Section G.** Stitch G1 to G2, trying to keep the edge adjacent to G4 straight. Straighten the edge before adding G3. Add G3, trying to keep the edge adjacent to G4 straight. Add G4, centering it on top of G1/G2/G3.

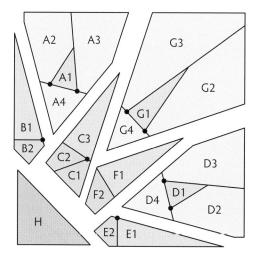

6. Straighten the edges before stitching one section to another section, making sure to only trim the edges you're sewing. Join the sections as follows.

- **Trim both A4 edges.** Join A and B, keeping the edge adjacent to C straight. Trim A/B, making sure you have a ¼" seam allowance at B2.
- **Add C to A/B,** matching the seam intersection for the circle at B2 and C2.

- **Trim both D4 edges.** Join D to E, keeping the edge adjacent to F straight. Trim D/E, making sure you have a ¼" seam allowance at E2.
- **Add F to D/E,** matching the seam intersection for the circle at E2 and F2.
- **Trim both G4 edges.** Add G to D/E/F, keeping the edge adjacent to C straight.
- **Trim A/B/C,** making sure you have a ¼" seam allowance at C2. Join A/B/C to D/E/F/G, matching the seam intersection for the circle at F2 and C2.
- **Add H,** centering the edge of H on the inner circle (B2, C1, C2, E2, and F2).

7. Repeat to make four matching quadrants for one block.

8. Trim the two inside edges of the quadrant as shown, positioning a ruler so that the seams for the inner circle (B2 and E2) are 2¾" from the upper-right corner as shown in step 9 on page 31. The points of the rays (B1 and E1) should be about 7" from the corner on the ruler, which gives you a ¼" seam allowance along the edge of the block after trimming. Your blocks may be larger or smaller, but pick consistent numbers for each set of four quadrants. For the circle to appear round and the points to match, it's important to use a consistent measurement for each set of four quadrants.

9. Join the quadrants, matching the center seam intersections and the seams for the inner circle. Try to match the sun points (B1 and E1) but don't worry if they don't match exactly.

10. Press and square up the block to measure 12½" x 12½".

11. Repeat to make a total of five blocks.

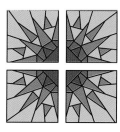 

Make 5.

MAKING THE PIECED OUTER BORDER

1. For the side units, place a light 2" square on one corner of a dark 3½" square. Sew diagonally from corner to corner as shown. Trim the excess corner fabric, leaving a ¼" seam allowance. Press the seam allowances toward the resulting triangle. In the same way, sew a light square on an adjacent corner. Trim and press to complete the unit. Make 104 units.

Make 104.

2. For the corner units, place a light 2" square on one corner of a dark 3½" square. Sew diagonally from corner to corner as shown. Trim the excess corner fabric, leaving a ¼" seam allowance. Press the seam allowances toward the resulting triangle. In the same way, sew a light square on the opposite corner. Trim and press to complete the unit. Make four units.

Make 4.

3. Join 26 units from step 1 side by side as shown in the quilt assembly diagram on page 87 to make a 78½"-long strip. Press the seam allowances in one direction. Make four strips.

4. Sew a corner unit to both ends of a strip from step 3 to make an 84½"-long strip for the top border. Repeat to make the bottom border.

ASSEMBLING THE QUILT TOP

1. Lay out the blocks, rust side triangles, and rust corner triangles in diagonal rows as shown in the quilt assembly diagram. Sew the blocks and side triangles together in rows. Press the seam allowances as indicated. Join the rows. Press the seam allowances in one direction. Add the corner triangles last and press. The quilt top should measure 68½" x 68½".

2. For the inner border, join the rust 5½"-wide strips end to end. From the pieced strip, cut two 68½"-long strips for the side borders and two 78½"-long strips for the top and bottom borders. Sew the side borders to the quilt top first, and then add the top and bottom borders. Press all seam allowances toward the inner border.

3. Sew the 26-unit outer-border strips to opposite sides of the quilt top. Add the top and bottom outer-border strips. Press all seam allowances toward the inner border.

FINISHING THE QUILT

If you need help with any of the following finishing tasks, go to ShopMartingale.com/HowtoQuilt for free, downloadable information. Layer the quilt top with batting and backing; baste. Hand or machine quilt as desired. Use the rust 2½"-wide strips to make and attach the binding.

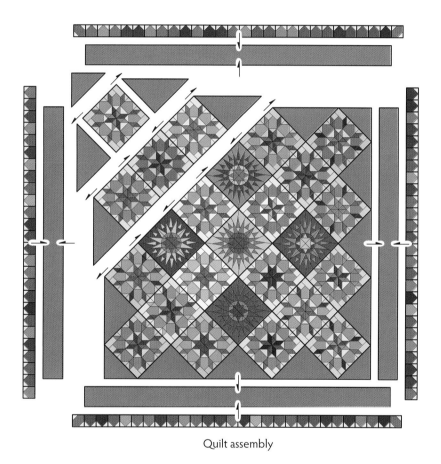

Quilt assembly

Cabins in the Pines

Granite Point on Loon Lake just north of Spokane, Washington, has been a summer destination for generations. My mom headed there with friends after high school graduation, my folks took us there for yearly Lions Club picnics, and now we take our kids to spend a crazy, fun-filled week every summer in our own cabin in the pines.

MATERIALS

Yardage is based on 42"-wide fabric. Fat quarters measure 18" x 21". Fat eighths measure 9" x 21".

8 fat quarters of assorted light or medium plaids or stripes for background (label as #1, #4, #6, #11, #12, #13, #16, and #17)

6 fat eighths of assorted light or medium plaids for background (label as #3, #5, #7, #8, #15, and #18)

⅛ yard *each* of 3 assorted light-cream plaids for background (label as #2, #9, and #10)

¼ yard of light or medium plaid for background (label as #14)

8 rectangles, 6" x 10", of assorted dark plaids for cabins

8 rectangles, 4" x 8", of assorted medium prints or plaids for cabin sides

8 rectangles, 3" x 5" of assorted dark-brown wools for roofs

8 rectangles, 2½" x 3½", of assorted light wools for cabin windows

8 rectangles, 2" x 4", of assorted wools for cabin doors

4 rectangles, 5" x 10", of assorted rust wools for chimneys

1 fat quarter (16" x 28") *each* of olive-green plaid and olive-green solid wools for large trees

5 rectangles, 7" x 8", of assorted dark-green wools for 5 small trees

1 rectangle, 14" x 16", of butter-yellow wool for moon and 1 large star

1 square, 7" x 7", *each* of 2 teal and 1 caramel wools for large stars

1 square, 4" x 4", *each* of 1 tan, 1 teal, and 1 cream wools for small stars

1¼ yards of green plaid for outer border

⅝ yard of dark-gray print for binding

3¼ yards of fabric for backing

58" x 66" piece of batting

3 yards of 16"-wide paper-backed fusible web

CUTTING

From *each* of the dark plaids for cabins, cut:
1 rectangle, 4½" x 8½"

From *each* of the assorted medium prints or plaids for cabin sides, cut:
1 rectangle, 2½" x 6½"

From background #1, cut:
1 rectangle, 12½" x 18½"

From background #2, cut:
1 rectangle, 4½" x 22½"
1 rectangle, 2½" x 6½"

From background #3, cut:
4 squares, 2½" x 2½"
1 rectangle, 6½" x 8½"

From background #4, cut:
1 rectangle, 10½" x 14½"

From background #5, cut:
1 square, 6½" x 6½"

Continued on page 90

Pieced by Gloria Brodhagen and quilted by Karen Brown.
Finished size: 52½" x 64½"

Continued from page 88

From background #6, cut:
    2 squares, 2½" x 2½"
    1 rectangle, 2½" x 6½"
    1 rectangle, 10½" x 14½"

From background #7, cut:
    1 rectangle, 6½" x 10½"

From background #8, cut:
    2 squares, 2½" x 2½"
    1 rectangle, 4½" x 8½"

From background #9, cut:
    1 rectangle, 4½" x 22½"

From background #10, cut:
    2 squares, 2½" x 2½"
    1 rectangle, 4½" x 26½"

From background #11, cut:
    1 square, 8½" x 8½"

From background #12, cut:
    1 rectangle, 8½" x 14½"

From background #13, cut:
    2 squares, 2½" x 2½"
    1 rectangle, 8½" x 10½"

From background #14, cut:
    1 rectangle, 6½" x 22½"

From background #15, cut:
2 squares, 2½" x 2½"
1 rectangle, 4½" x 8½"

From background #16, cut:
1 rectangle, 10½" x 12½"

From background #17, cut:
1 rectangle, 10½" x 12½"

From background #18, cut:
2 squares, 2½" x 2½"
1 rectangle, 6½" x 10½"

From the green plaid, cut:
6 strips, 6½" x 42"

From the dark-gray, cut:
7 strips, 2½" x 42"

MAKING THE CABIN BLOCKS

1. Lay out the background pieces as shown in the quilt assembly diagram on page 92. Choose the color placement for each cabin; the background of the Cabin blocks will be the same as the adjacent background fabric (see the photo on page 90). Once you've determined the background for each of the cabins, place a matching background 2½" square on the top corner of a cabin side 2½" x 6½" rectangle. Sew diagonally from corner to corner as shown. Trim the excess corner fabric, leaving a ¼" seam allowance. Press the seam allowance toward the resulting triangle. Make five left cabin sides and three right cabin sides.

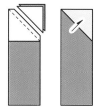
Make 5
right cabin sides.

Make 3
left cabin sides.

2. To complete the Cabin block, stitch a matching background 2½" square to the top of a cabin side. Then sew the Cabin side to a cabin 4½" x 8½" rectangle. Make five blocks with cabin sides on the right and three blocks with cabin sides on the left.

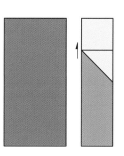
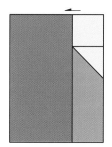
Make 5.

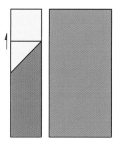
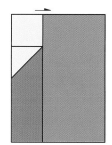
Make 3.

ASSEMBLING THE QUILT TOP

1. Sew the background pieces together to make the top half. Then sew the pieces together to make the bottom half. Wait to join the two halves until after the appliqué is complete.

2. Referring to "Fusible Wool Appliqué" on page 11 and using the patterns on pages 93 and 95, cut out the chimney, roof, door, and windows on each cabin from the appropriate wools. Using matching thread, whipstitch the motifs in place. Be sure to reverse the motifs for blocks with the cabins on the left side.

3. Using the patterns on pages 93–95 and the appropriate wools, cut out the trees, stars, and moon. Using matching thread, whipstitch the motifs in place as shown in the photo on page 90.

4. Stitch the two halves of the quilt together and complete any overlapping appliqué.

5. Join three green-plaid 6½"-wide strips end to end. Repeat to make a second pieced strip. From each pieced strip, cut one 40½"-long strip for the top and bottom borders and one 60½"-long strip for the side borders. Sew the top and bottom borders to the quilt top first, and then add the side borders. Press all seam allowances toward the border.

FINISHING THE QUILT

If you need help with any of the following finishing tasks, go to ShopMartingale.com/HowtoQuilt for free, downloadable information. Layer the quilt top with batting and backing; baste. Hand or machine quilt as desired. Use the dark-gray 2½"-wide strips to make and attach the binding.

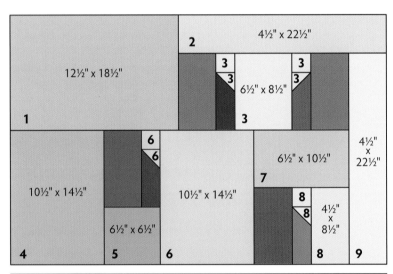

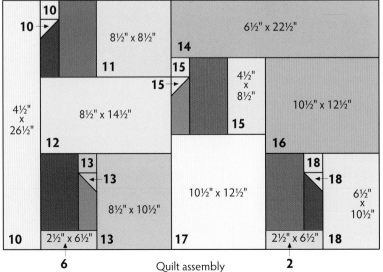

Quilt assembly

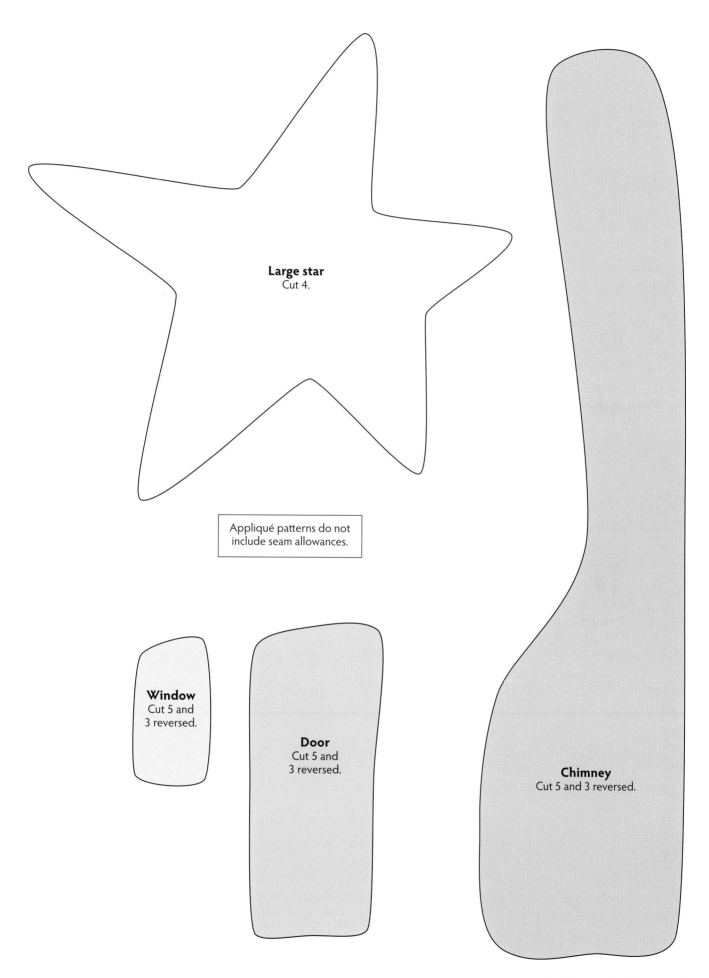

Large star
Cut 4.

Appliqué patterns do not
include seam allowances.

Window
Cut 5 and
3 reversed.

Door
Cut 5 and
3 reversed.

Chimney
Cut 5 and 3 reversed.

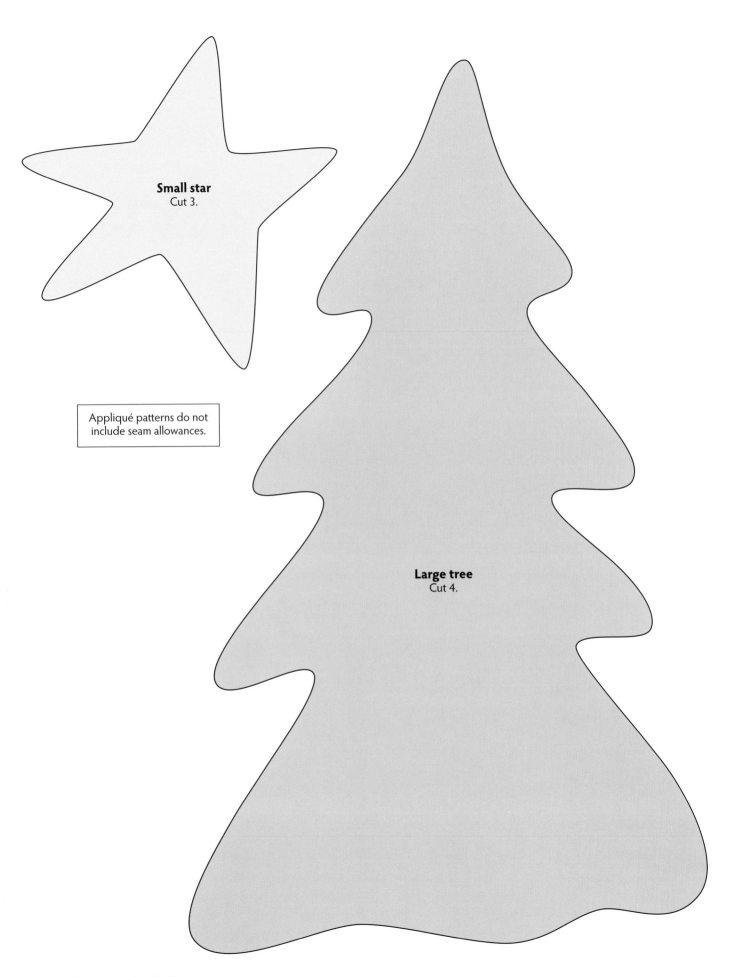

Small star
Cut 3.

Appliqué patterns do not
include seam allowances.

Large tree
Cut 4.

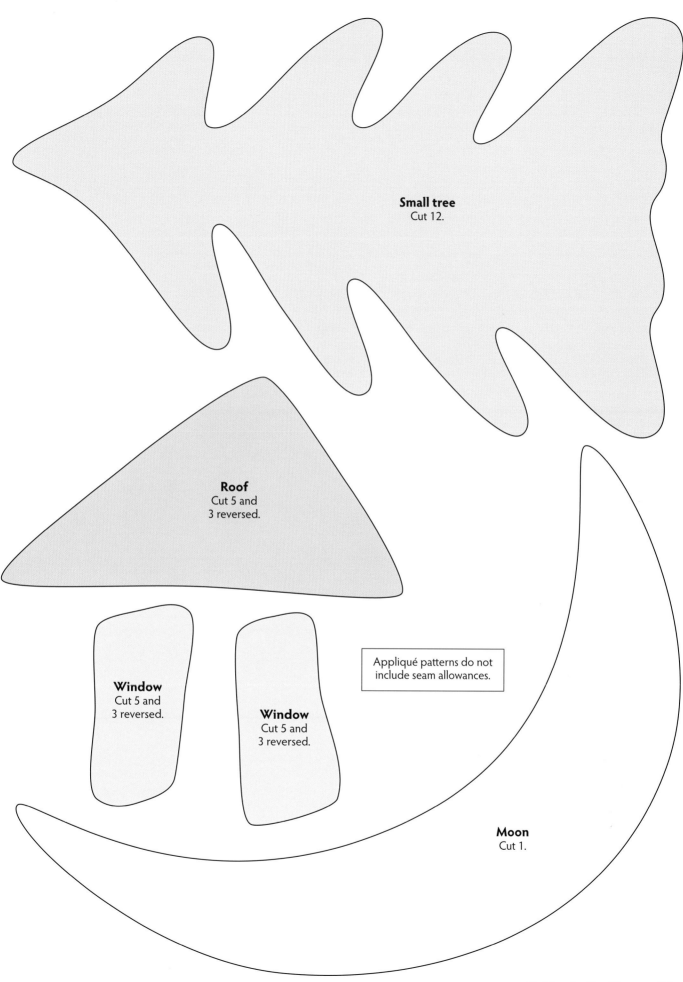

Small tree
Cut 12.

Roof
Cut 5 and
3 reversed.

Window
Cut 5 and
3 reversed.

Window
Cut 5 and
3 reversed.

Appliqué patterns do not
include seam allowances.

Moon
Cut 1.

ABOUT THE AUTHOR

Janet Nesbitt is a quilt and fabric designer and the owner of One S1ster LLC, a web-based quilt-design company. For 18 years, she owned and operated Buggy Barn Quilts in Reardan, Washington, and designed the popular Buggy Barn line of quilt patterns and Henry Glass & Co. fabric collections. Now, she has a new adventure well underway as One S1ster, where she continues to design both quilt patterns and fabric for Henry Glass & Co.

Janet has always been an avid scrap quilter with a passion for mixing prints and plaids that incorporate a unique sense of color. In this new phase in her career, she is enjoying focusing more of her time on creating fun and whimsical designs through her popular Crazy piecing technique (stacking fabric, cutting the lines, shuffling, and stitching it all together). Janet takes pleasure in sharing quilt patterns that inspire creativity and put a smile on quilters' faces.

onesisterdesigns.com
onesisterdesigns.blogspot.com
onesisterdesigns@gmail.com

ACKNOWLEDGMENTS

Thank you to my friends who rallied around and spent their summer helping me prepare this book for you to enjoy. I absolutely couldn't have done it without their efforts and cheerful support. They remain the best. My piecers, Sandi McKell and Gloria Brodhagen, and machine quilters, Karen Brown and Kathy Woods, literally made this book happen! Thank you from deep within my "crazy" heart!